# THE DIARY OF AN UNEMPLOYED GENTLEMAN

*A NOVEL That Isn't*

*By*

## ELIAS SASSOON

ISBN: 978-1470155568

The Diary Of An Unemployed Gentleman: A NOVEL That Isn't

First Printing: March 2012

# DEDICATION

To my late mother. She was a woman who hardly understood me, but supported my every move. Your backing is missed very much.

# TABLE OF CONTENTS

# DIARY OF AN UNEMPLOYED GENTLEMAN

## INTRODUCTION TO DAYS OF UNEMPLOYMENT WONDER

What do we have here? This volume, what does it consist of? Nonfiction? Fiction? Philosophy? Drama? Who knows? Who cares. What we do know is basically this: We have a man of the twentieth and twenty-first century who has attempted to put down his daily thoughts in a diary of sorts, but no ordinary diary of sorts of any sorts. What we have here then is a mental diary, or, the diary of somebody who is mental, a diary of the daily thoughts of the mental (case), rather than a diary of the daily actions of the mental (case). It is the diary of a neurotic, as you shall see, and the neurotic is a neurotic precisely because he is not a man of action, not a person of physicality of any sort, just a person whose main exercise is conjecture, speculation, philosophical discourse, obsessive questioning about self, his-self, my-self. Who is he? Let us just say, he, I, he, no me, he is a sportsman of his own mind, my mind. What is the sport that the sportsman is engaged in or within? Well, that sport is not out-gaining an opponent by swinging a bat or throwing a ball, not that type of sport; the sport is called figuring, that is, figuring out how he, me, he got to that moment in time and then questioning his questions. What is the end point of the neurosis?

Putting it down, writing it that is, writing about the daily mental grind that comes about because of being unemployed in an employed world. It is almost the equivalent of being an alien in a human world, or a common plant with blue-colored foliage in a world where green predominates. It is an important topic, this unemployment thing, and that's why I am writing about it, my thoughts about it. Important, yes! Think about it, the job, importance, having it, a must for all of us these days. The job is not just a job; having the job is not only the means of earning the paycheck, but also the means of socializing with your fellow citizens, a method of participation in group activities; in general, it is the way to get connected. Being without, being isolated in the suburbs of houses - I am presently located in some suburban place existing beyond time - without personality, deserted streets, distant shopping malls, etc., etc., etc., there is no connection, no joining. What is the result of this? What effects does it have on the individual facing the isolation, facing the unemployment? You grow out of touch and then grow out of your mind, the mind retreating into the distant past or the distant future, the mind trying not to stay in the present moment for fear of that present moment.

But, this unemployment thing that has hit home, hit me, hits a lot of others sooner or later, does present us, me, us with an opportunity. Being given the boot by my now ex-employer is some stroke of luck, some sign from heaven or hell, good, good, great, good, and so we, I, we classify it as an opportunity. It allows me, the unemployment thing, allows me and all who care, to understand what it means to be on the outside looking in, it allows me to feel the pain in the pit of my stomach, pain that comes from not knowing what will happen to you, the pain of wondering. It is terrible thing to feel that pain but also the greatest privilege on earth. Pain is hell but hell is liberating, got that, caught that, better have gotten and caught that.

So the following pages have my pain, and through it, others can understand, and maybe others can be helped. I think that is a possibility but I am unsure of this conclusion. Remember, anybody that tells you they are sure of something, anything, is either a liar or trying to sell you something. This is the wholesome truth of the matter, and if not the wholesome truth, the perverted truth twisted towards normalcy.

**JUNE  2001**

# WEEK 1

## Tuesday, June 5, 2001

Day, unemployment comes. Let's discuss this, talk about it, understand how it all transpired that on this Tuesday afternoon, an afternoon like no other when there is no other, I am fired, laid off, given the proverbial boot. How can this happen to one so perfect as I, I, Cyrus - just call me Cy - Nishani, a great decent man of the world, giving, caring, loving, and all that other horseradish bilge spit out for public consumption by a human without a public and without a consumption.

Laid off of a job that I was never born to do, that I, in fact, was meant to be laid off from. That is the key; the job, from which I was expunged, was a job which had absolutely no meaning to myself. When we speak of no meaning, we speak of lifeless, idea-less, without a sound reason for being, a job whose only purpose was to employ a body so that the body could earn a check so that the body could be a consumer in the Western marketplace of supply and demand and various other ideas that are GNP related but never humanitarian related.

A job, is that what I said, yes, I had a job and I was removed from it today but a woman, middle class like myself, overly dressed, overly perfumed, wearing eye shadow and lipstick, wearing a fine, gray cotton dress, hair nicely done - it is always nicely done - and with this ID bracelet around her wrist; is the bracelet made of white gold or is it silver. There is a difference you know between white gold and silver; you know that, of course. It has to do with price. Gold is more expensive than silver; consequently, owning gold makes you richer than owning silver. It is all about investment grades and investment values and protecting yourself against old age and the poverty of being old, monetary poverty and mental poverty. So here is this woman from the company where I worked - no, not worked; just hung around would be the better term - and she is the one that expunges me. She represents Personnel at the company and is sometimes referred to as the Human Resources woman. She calls me on the phone this day and summons me to her office on another floor. She is at her door when I arrive, smiling tersely, her green eyes glaring at me. I enter her office and she closes the door. I sit down at her table. She pulls out some papers. She smiles at me; I smile at her. The moment has arrived. She shoves the papers at me.

"We have decided. . . ."

She uses the term 'We' to describe the company, I know, but I find the term 'We' when used to describe oneself, terribly inappropriate. Why do people associate themselves with institutions anyway? Does that make them feel more important, more like God's gift instead of silly little human animals that wander the planet aimlessly looking for meaning when there is no meaning to be found anywhere? Now, does that sound dour, cynical, pessimistic, and depressed? Maybe, yes, maybe no. But that collective term, it just turns my stomach drastically. And, not only for the reason I mentioned, no, no, no, no. When 'We' use the word 'We,' we think that gives us justification to commit the worst crimes and misdemeanors. We can commit war and murder by using the term 'We;' we can screw our brothers and sisters by using the word 'We.' We can play God using the word 'We.' What kind of crap is that!

"We have decided that the job you do no longer fits what is required. Unfortunately, you have become overqualified for the position." The nicely dressed and good smelling Personnel lady gives me a slight grin and raises her thin cheeks in an attempt at a smile, or, is it a look of pity; see how her plucked eyebrows are changing direction. "We have prepared this document for you to sign that clears us of all liability. Oh, but I see that you are a little apprehensive, but don't be."

"But, how will signing this, effect my unemployment insurance. I will need to collect."

Ah, there we go, me being totally practical about a matter of practicality. But why not? At this point, I am not shocked, couldn't care less, just seek to understand where my next dollar bill is coming from and ensure that I continue to collect dollar bills into the future. That's all this adds up to, this employment business, wampum changing hands continually, the job gives me the wampum and I then turn around and give other people the wampum and then the cycle repeats. It is sort of like eating and shitting and going to bed and getting up in the morning. Repeating cycles that end only with death - do I sound like some philosophical schmuck, well that's because I am one.

"Signing the form will not affect your ability to collect Unemployment in any way. But read it over first just to make sure. Then you can sign it." As I begin my reading of the words on the white paper, the Personnel Lady, whose given or Christian name - I forget which - is Betty, shuffles some other papers she has there in readiness for whatever, whenever. I admire her professionally, maybe even her clinical approach to my removal from the work-a-day world. How calm and dispassionate she is; she'd make a good doctor, maybe a brain surgeon who remains emotionally distant when digging into somebody's cranium. Is that a good analogy? Maybe not! How about another one, a Nazi who smiles dispassionately when escorting young adults into gas chambers and then ransacks the dead, bloated bodies for valuables thereafter. No. Bad analogy. This woman, Betty, is certainly no Nazi and she certain is no brain surgeon. She is merely this human being who is married with two kids and lives in a meticulous house on Long Island - a suburb of suburbs - and who merely wants some sort of order in her life, to eat and sleep normally, to have her kids and husband eat and sleep normally, to copulate with her husband once or twice a week, to have her parents over and friends over for barbecues once or twice a summer, to have Christmas presents and Christmas trees during the season, to go off on one week vacations to New England or California or the Bahamas or on a cruise to nowhere once or twice a year, to go to that Wedding or that confirmation or that party and dress up three or four times a year, that's all for Betty. An ordered world, that is Betty's world, Betty the Personnel

Lady. So what is it about Betty? She's not bad or good. She is neutral or neuter, just seeking to get along without any of the pain that might come about in life. This is understandable.

"Everything looks like it is in order, Betty. I can sign the form now." I take a pen and prepare to sign away my life on the doted line.

"No, not yet Cyrus. We need to have another witness." Betty calls in her assistant, an equally innocuous woman, nicely dressed in a red cotton dress. I notice her high heels and her pearl necklace for some reason; in fact, my eyes fasten onto the pearls themselves; are they Tahitian? I must be going mad if that's all I can think about at a time like this. "Suzie, we need you to counter-sign the termination form." Betty tells her assistant.

Suzie is all smiles. "Sure, great, okay! Where do you want me to sign? Nice to see you Cyrus. You look good." Suzie signs the form, I sign the form, Betty signs the form and dates the form and we all smile, as Suzie disappears from the scene. "Well goodbye Cyrus and good luck. Take care."

I smile and wave and think nothing of it. I won't miss Suzie; she won't miss me. In a few weeks, we might pass one another on the street and not know it. Why should I remember her or care to remember her. Why should I form an opinion on the Suzie's of the world? Why should I form an opinion on the Suzie's of the world? Why waste energy on people like that, those who are not capable of returning real concerns. It is like caring for a rock and basing your life on a rock's feelings when a rock cannot have feelings. A rock is a rock and those that love the rock and expect to be loved by the rock are fools plain and simple or simple and very plain.

"Now then Cy, we have more forms for you to fill out. Though will no longer be with us, by law you are still entitled to keep the company's medical and dental plans under COBRA. Here are the COBRA forms, which you must fill out and sent to the insurance company as soon as possible. Of course, you understand that the company no longer will be picking up the payments. If you choose to go with COBRA, you must pay the monthly premiums out of pocket, which can be sizeable. You may wish to do that, however, as you have a family and. . . ."

Talking and talking, round and round about forms, insurance companies, government regulations, more forms, and when Betty gets through with that, then it's the pension plan and forms to fill out, forms from the company, the government, Betty, forms, smiling, impersonal, helpful, into the pit you go and here are the forms to cushion your fall.

"Now, do you understand everything?" Betty asks after the endless succession of words and bureaucratic red-tape. I nod, but in reality, I understand very little of what she has said. But that isn't that odd now because I barely understand what anybody in life says or tries to say. People say that I tune out, but that's a lie, a dirty lie. I never turned in. I don't like any of the channels; their frequencies hurt my ears. You want the real truth; I purposely exclude all thoughts that do not directly pertain to my: eating, sleeping, excreting, and copulating. Other things, various thoughts, ideologies, man-made equations do not concern me.

"Well I am glad we finished that," Betty informs me, pursing her skinny lips that match her skinny body. I look a little bit closer to her face and notice that she has slight blotches on her cheeks. I bet she has some sort of skin disease. "Now, I must escort you out of our building; it is our policy. Why don't we go downstairs to your desk and we can collect your belongings. Won't that be nice?"

I nod. "Nice, sure, you are going to escort me. But, but, I really don't want my co-workers, now former co-workers to know. I don't want to be embarrassed."

Betty gives me a broader smile. "Of course not, Cyrus, I understand. I will escort you downstairs and stand in the background while you collect your things. I'll be as inconspicuous as possible. Don't worry about anything."

Worry, me, I. I smile back now and enter Betty's la-la-land where reality is not reality and evil is not evil, where evil doesn't exist and where bad things just happen but are not really bad. Now does that make sense?

So, here we go, Betty has her forms now, I have my forms now, and she is escorting me down to the first floor to my desk which I have inhabited for the past year and a half. As we voyage down in the elevator, Betty turns to me and says, "How is your family doing? You have a son and a daughter, right. I met your son once; you brought him in. He was very nice." I answer that my family is doing well, although shortly they may not be without suitable income to buy them the essentials of life. "Good, glad, nice, the best. Kids are great aren't they? I have two teenage daughters of my own. What a handful they are."

We get to my floor. As promised, Betty hangs back, while I corral the papers on my desk, bag things and carry things out. It is past 5:00 p.m. and many of my co-workers are gone. To the few that remain, I pretend nonchalance. I haven't really collected much in a year in a half, a few papers here, a few there, a book here, a pencil there, and a paper clip there. And soon, I half-fill a shopping bag and soon Betty is escorting me to the front door and to the end of the line.

"Well, Cyrus, it has been good. Good luck to you and have a great life. If you have any questions later about the forms we discussed, feel free to give me a call."

I thank Betty and wave goodbye as I hit the parking lot. She is already gone, turned away, up the elevator.

Bye, bye Betty. Bye, bye, company.

### Wednesday, June 6, 2001

In retrospect, everything in retrospect, getting up in the morning as an unemployed adult seeking adults that are employed. The wife going to work as a school teacher; the kids going to school as students, and me alone in the house in the suburbs amidst an absence of life, maybe an absence of humanity. Only the squirrels are here to keep me company.

Here, in the house, alone but not contemplating the job or missing the job. I am only contemplating the money and what it means to not be earning it anymore, or, at least temporally. What to do? How to do it? Questions and more questions, but the job, the people. How can I miss the job? You see, the job to me is just that, a job and not a career and there is a difference, and we can call that passion. Difference, job, career, career, job. You are supposed to love your career; you are supposed to hate your job. A career is supposed to be your avocation, your job is supposed to be your paycheck. But then again, is this really true, I mean really. When does the career become the job? The answer, the career becomes a job as soon as you start earning money for it, as soon as the boss begins barking at you, as soon as your customers begin complaining, as soon as the wife and kids demand more money, the career becoming the job. I don't know, maybe this is a bit too cynical, maybe, possibly. I don't know everything, you know, you do know that, right?

All of this raises another question, what is the difference between the career and the profession? What does it mean to be a professional or to be truly professional? How about the term the helping profession. Now there is a term for you. I guess - I like guessing, don't you - the term equates to people with licenses that give them a right to do a certain job; we are back to the idea of job again. Okay, fair, nice. But what type of licenses, doctor, lawyer, teacher, hair dresser, plumber, electrician? Yeah, and there are millions of more licenses to boot, giving people the right to do a job. Licenses of a profession, of a professional, a helping professional, and this might be good, helping, the idea of working at a profession, at a career, that translates into a job and helping others while you are doing that. Maybe that's the key, being able to help, being able to add to human life or life in general. Thing of the professional that is the Forest Ranger, he is helping the animal population, the same for the veterinarian or the zoo keeper, etc. How about the botanist helping plants grow, helping flowers bloom. How nice this is or at least is in theory. To actually put something back into life, to add to it, how great is that. But, how many do that? How many add to life? On the contrary, can we ask, how many people add nothing? How many just live for the sake of existing? Is that good, bad or something in between. To live just to live, to eat, have sex, excrete waste products, breathe in general for no other reason but to eat, have sex, excrete waste products, breathe, is that worth it. Is the goal not to be a helping professional? But how many are helping professional.

Go outside the lines then, outside the Profession, Career, Job thing, and what do you have. Can people not add to life outside these categories? What of religion, being moral, presenting a moral compass in the world, each one presenting a moral compass in this everlasting world. Theoretically, but I have been out in the world where religion is in that world and for the most part people exist and religion exists but rarely do they meet up. Maybe they meet on holidays, on occasions like birth and death and the like and marriage and confirmations and the like, but rarely thereafter. Again, most people just want to just not been bothered; they want to eat, use the toilet bowl, copulate, sleep, on a continuous basis and ask few questions. They don't want to add to life, nor, do they wish to detract from life. They are the majority, silent, not ever seeking to be the difference makers like politicians who seek to be helping professionals, but often times just become professionals who seek to help only themselves.

Which is where I come in. I am one of those that eats, sleeps, copulates, excretes on a continuous basis, but secretly craves to add some substance to life, but can never find the right vehicle through which to add. I am part of the multitudes that add nothing; but am part of the few who want to add. When younger the thought of becoming a teacher, a helping professional of children, but somehow they got waylaid by thoughts of becoming a great writer of things. A great writer of things in a helping profession, that's what I thought then, when I was young. I would write to change the world, to improve it beyond its current condition, the world it is, I would write to make people think and laugh and write to raise them from ignorance and poverty, anyway, that was the plan, or the thought, which has proved to be something very different than that. I did my part, wrote and wrote and wrote and turned out the words on paper but nobody would ever read what I wrote, not family, friends, publishers, anybody. I could never earn a living writing and making a living from being a helping professional, and thus I turned to jobs, sitting at desks in cubicles, in office buildings, in big cities mostly and occasionally in the suburbs. Taking the job, not the career, not the profession, but never giving up the idea of being that helping professional that might change the world, or at least give something to it, never giving up the idea of writing and having the words translate to the common man. Never giving up the idea, and writing by night with that idea, I writing, nightly, something at lunch, sometimes at breakfast, sneaking the writing in, I, myself.

Being laid off yesterday, and I feel not much. How many jobs have I had in the past twenty-five years? Twenty-five or thereabouts, never amounting to much, never adding up to anything. I wonder about people and the jobs they have had, not the professions, not those with careers, I wonder about most of us, I wonder what they take away from years and years of jobs? I ask that question but I know the answer. They take away a sense of having lived through it, pride in getting through it, pride in paying for the house and the cars and putting the kids through school and getting a little pension together. But what about the jobs themselves? They usually speak little about that. That was never important. Function, like taking a leak or a dump, something that they did. There is little pride in the job, little pride in being a white-collar somewhere and pushing papers across a padded desk, little pride in manipulating numbers at a computer terminal. There is little of any of it. They might take some pride in having made a few friends, in the personal about the job and there is a personal in a job because the job is made up of people. Yet, people at a job are their for the most part as cogs in the wheel, the wheel being the business run by a boss or bosses or board of director bosses. Cogs have little rights, usually, cogs can form office friends only at the convenience of the boss or bosses and are always subject to the boss or bosses manipulations. Cogs can be turned against one another or toward one another, cogs can be disposed of, disgraced, humiliated, and thus the job itself is not the best breeding ground of friendship that the world ever invented. But friendship can occur at the job and can last after the job is over, which always happens. But even there, how many friendships are based on being there, at the job, like rats in a cage that pair up only because they are trapped together in a cage and there is nothing better for them to do. When the cage breaks or disappears and the inhabitants are released they flee their separate ways and thus, the friends united by ties of bondage are released forever and a day.

Job as a cage, and almost Job as a jail, but never quite because unlike a jail you can always quit the job and face poverty and hunger and desperation, get kicked out of your apartment, divorce your wife/husband, abandon your children because of financial pressures, get threatened by the bank because of the mortgage payments and the credit card companies and the various other bill collectors who still need to get paid despite you quitting your job. So you have a choice of quitting, of course you do and voluntarily abandoning your cage called the job. Of course, you have a choice, so the cage is not a jail after all. Or, is it?

Sad but true, true but sad, and sadder to say that I did not understand any of these basic concepts years ago. I was a moron years ago, a fool walking to hell and thinking it was really to Hawaii where I was headed. Nut, jerk, baboon, idiot, other names for me at that time, at that period of my life when I had left college for real life in the real world where everything is make believe and trumped up. And now I want to tell you why I was this freaking and flaming idiot: the reason fellow Romans is that I actually approached a job as a matter of personal pride and accomplishment, I actually put myself into a job and took the whole thing to heart. Even if I was pushing papers and pushing buttons at a job whose object was always unclear, I tried my best and somehow felt this sense of pride and was always looking for compliments from co-workers and bosses and the like. Boy, did I get lots of odd looks from older employees who knew the real score and did I ever get some sleazy smirks from bosses who saw in me a young duckling who could be manipulated by praise or the absence thereof. Everything I took personally, every remark about my work I took personally, personally well or personally bad and in the end reacted to everything personally and in the end was forced to leave the premises (when I was young I was rarely asked to leave any premises; I always left of my own accord;

later, as I grew older and wiser and was not such a bonus to any growing corporation looking for flesh blood, I was rushed out the door by various people using various approaches.). How dumb was I, people tried to tell me to not personalize the job, that the job did not matter in the long run, but I wouldn't listen as I was beyond comprehension. To have one's self-worth hooked into a job is grounds for the ultimate disaster, which is feeling bad about yourself. And, in that time, I always felt bad. Now it seems so simple, the job is a paycheck, the paycheck is a job. It is almost monotheistic-like, there is only one God and we are his subjects, if you believe in monotheism; but even that people confuse, lose, and get consumed and weird about. Jobs, people who know, they confuse themselves sometimes, make things more complicated than they really should be, just like religion.

Jobs, money making, the masses, just going through the motions for that paycheck, it is a mere formality like eating, shitting, sleeping, etc. We've discussed that already, have we not! But those who know, those who forget, the real nature of the job, get involved in the job, begin to think the job is them, that they are the job when they are just the hired hand; confusion abounding, politics at the job, worker turned against worker, the complications profound. Job and workers, workers vying for promotions, workers vying for raises, workers vying to kiss the bosses ass, vying and forgetting that it is a job and not some life altering mission. Sad, all delusional and in the end leading to nothing.

### Thursday, June 7, 2001

I am still not losing track of days which is what happens when you are out of work and the rest of the world is working. The days move, pass, and blur. But this is only a couple days since I was gainfully employed at a place in the suburbs so things aren't blurred yet and I still not the time of day and the date of day. I guess I have to start thinking about registering for Unemployment, that is, registering to get my weekly check which is paid out through the mail once a week and which will be continued to be paid out for 26 weeks in a row. It's not such a bad thing except that initial applying business, going down to the government's office, meeting clerks, waiting on lines, looking at bulletin boards of happily productive people, listing to stories of my fellow unemployed, wondering if I am like them, forming more lines, being directed into other lines, filling out forms, being told I am filling out the wrong form and that I am in the wrong lines, waiting your turn, waiting my turn, going up to the clerks, being looked at with pity or with indifference, being questioned about what lead to the unemployment, on and on and on, inside the dark unemployment office with dingy fluorescent lighting haphazardly displayed, and the air smelling of death disinfected by old newspapers. Hate the thought of applying, driving to the building in the middle of a slum of a little town that is a slum. I can't do it today. I will do it next week. There is time to do that next week. There is also time next week to start to look for a job, any job. Next week, I like the idea of next week or the week after next week, putting it off, I like that idea. Good idea, Cyrus.

### Friday, June 8, 2001

The world and my unemployment, today that comes to the fore, how to deal with the world when you are first unemployed, how to explain it to the world. But, who the freak is the world anyway and why am I so concerned. Will the world be worried about me when I am under the ground and long-ago rotted? Who will remember or care that I was unemployed at one period of my forgotten life or another. Which brings up appearances, who the freak (short for another profanity) cares for this idea? I certainly don't. Appearances, keeping them up, so to speak. Why? Peer pressure appearances and keeping them up, up with appearances, appearances up everybody, everybody up with appearances.

Now, if my theory is correct, there should be little reason to have to be up with appearances. What is that theory? My friends, that theory is as clear as the egg upon your dimpled faces, that theory, everybody, every human thinks they are the asshole of the world, got it, have it, enjoy it. Asshole as in center or centered or central or in the middle of, or as in, the life of the party or as in the sun in the solar system and the like. Nobody cares a crap except when that crap has a bearing upon them, and when it does, then they force it to have a bearing on you and it is called peer pressure. Job, who cares if you have a job or not except that their thinking, the world is thinking, if he doesn't have a job, why should I have a job. Or, if he doesn't have a job that means he is having a good time, and if he's having a good time, I should have a good time and I'm not having a good time on the job. How dare that son of a bitch have a good time? Thus, peer pressure comes in and with peer pressure often comes the advice. "Cy, why don't you try to apply for a teaching job?" Or, "CY, I know what you can do, look for a government job." Advice from peers to the unemployed here, the words, made so that I do not rock their boat, that I don't have a good time while they are having a miserable time. Peers, peers, everywhere, and that is what the hell I am thinking about today, a Friday of my unemployment.

Jealousy and envy, human characteristics, not having a job, envious, by coming through as pity or coming through as being judgmental, envy, peers are envious, human beings are envious, stupidly so. Do not feed into it, into the nonsense. But it can be difficult, very difficult, not feeding into it even when you know the reason for it, for their nonsense; knowledge is not always power, power is not always wanted. You know something but can't change something so you suffer twice as much. Isn't that true! Living with peers, conforming to their wants and desires is very difficult to try to maneuver around. I try, and as I grow older, I try a little harder. But the only way to really do it is to play the game of pretend, that is, pretend they are not there and that they were never there, the way to also do it is cut them off, the society around you, the friends around you, the acquaintances around you, the family around you, the strangers around you who constitute your peers. Do not let them in, do not confide, or chide or tell of your longings of despair. Cutting off the peers before the peers cut you off. Alienation, yes, that is a consequence, but you must be brave. There is a price to be paid for everything and everything has a price.

When did I first learn about peers and the pressure they apply, peers and the part they play in getting a person to conform to the whims of society, to a society that is moved by economic factors that call for people to produce, to purchase, to purchase, to produce, for people to work, to produce, to buy, everybody must produce and buy, work to produce and buy, that is the way of the society and that is the way of peers and peer pressure. It is all such a trap, or better said, walls that are closing in, that ring you, press you, make you fidget; it is always there, the pressure to conform, to be employed, to remain employed, the pressure to work, produce and buy. Peers everywhere sent out like soldiers by government and economic organizations everywhere. Again, when did I first learn about this peer pressure as a force of manipulation? In college of course, when I talked to my fellow young people, or, we may call them, my fellow young dopes. Peer pressure in the form of question, "Cyrus, so what is your major? History, what will you do with history? Are there many jobs in the field? I am going out for law. There are many jobs for lawyers right now."

Jobs and talk of getting them while I was sitting there in an educational setting. To me the educational setting was a place where I was supposed to learn and not earn. Ruining it for me with their thoughts and worries. Learning for me was a pure thing, clean thing without economic incentive. Learn for learning sake; do not learn for others sake, for money's sake. Pressure, peer pressure to become economically viable in one's studies, that was the thing. Always talking, directing, and controlling the mind. How sick, how depressing. I learned though, learned to avoid peer-dome, learned to live in my own world, for the most part. It is all a mater of being or becoming a loner.

Tomorrow comes the weekend and my wife and kids will be home for two days and I will have a temporary break from my isolation.                                                                                                     Bravo!

*WEEK 2*

## Monday, June 11, 2001

Monday morning and everybody is out of the house and I am alone again. The weekend went so quickly. What did we do? Ask my wife, the director of operations, to dinner, to shopping malls, to taking the kids to parties, to going out on a barbecue at my sisters, to visiting my wife's parents in the city, on and on, and me following and feeling good following because I am generally very alone and generally never know what to do physically in this world. If I am not directed, I just sit there and allow the world to spin about without me. I have always been this way, never knowing what to do and never seeing relevance in doing anything. I can sit there and sit there and sit there and while I sit there, I think about doing something, anything but I can't think of anything to do or that I want to do. And while I sit there, I think and think and think and question what is wrong with me and what is wrong with the world and why I am so out of step.

So here I am alone today in suburbia, in a suburban setting, in a two story house on a deserted side-street and there is absolutely no cars or people in sight. Any kid that lives here is in school, and any adult is at work, at the job, at the office, or, whatever, you want to call it; the adult is working to pay off the mortgage and working to pay for the school and real estate taxes of the town, thousands of dollars upon which are also the gas and electric bills, the water bills, telephone and Internet bills, cable bills, bills, bills, working for bills, the job for bills, paying the bills, so you can live in a house that is completely isolated and generally without merit emotionally, artistically or in any other way normal, good or satisfactory.

Being isolated after a weekend being with my two kids and listening to them screaming with one another and demanding of one another and demanding of me and my wife, demands, screams, wants, desires, needs, material, food, toys, sharing, yelling, being directed by the wife, having the wife speaking to me constantly, warning me, asking me, telling me we have to go, being alone after, now, being unemployed and isolated, it is definitely a strange feeling and much stranger than fiction. It is strange being isolated all day during the week and then having my kids and wife (the schoolteacher) coming in the door at 3:30 p.m. and listing to the uproar after hours and hours of sterile quiet. The mind must be trained not to sit through the isolation of hours of the day waiting for the uproar of the late afternoon. Isolation, you have to learn it, learn to appreciate it, embrace it and there is always the relearning process. You can learn to appreciate the isolation, but when you are away from it for a certain amount of time, you forget how to deal with it and all that comes with it, mostly thoughts, mainly regrets.

But it is amazing how many people cannot be alone, cannot exist in isolation. I remember this young man at the last job, where I was rudely given the boot/door/stab in the back, we'll call him Dennis, and he once told me how he couldn't be alone. "I've been in therapy for the past fifteen years trying to deal with that issue," Dennis - in his late thirties - confided in me. "I just can't be alone with myself; that's what makes me so needy and neurotic and that's what's driving my girlfriend away - I love her so much that I can't tell you in words. She's a doctor and very busy and made more busy because she's got a kid from a previous marriage, but I can't stand when she's away from me, I can't stand being alone in my apartment. I get nervous, I get depressed and I can't do it. I can't." Dennis would tell me all this at least once or twice a day, he was that type of guy, but I always had trouble believing him. I'd hear him on the phone with his girlfriend begging for her to give him some time that night or the next night, begging for quality time, fighting with her for that time, crying with her for that time, pleading with her not to abandon him, that he'd try harder to be more independent. I heard, everybody in the company heard his pleas and shook their head. And finally, I began believing Dennis and understanding his inability to be alone and isolated, isolated and alone, which may or may not be two separate issues. But when I have thought about it, I mean about Dennis and his fears, there are many people like this, fearful of being alone, fearful of finding themselves deserted in a cold, harsh world of their own making. How many people have told me just that about the alone thing, how many have questioned my love of going out for myself, existing in the world myself, performing activities myself - movies, jogging, traveling - alone, completely unburdened by others.

To be alone is to be free. You are unburdened by human rules and regulations. You exist in a world all your own. There are no rules but your rules, rules not shared with others; how good is that. Yes, you can never share those rules, the personal ones, because others will attempt to discredit and tear them to pieces. Alone, embracing the freedom to create your own world, your own government, your own army and navy, your own economic system. You are a civilization all your own. Then again, being alone does not mean you have to be isolated. You can be alone and interacting with others in some manner or form. Being alone is like doing your own thing but respecting the plight of others. Isolated means you are cut off from others and traveling outside the solar system in limitless space and time, which can be downright irritating or downright alienating, although, I imagine you can learn to enjoy that state, floating above it all, floating in a universe without any sort of gravitation pull. This state, however, may put you, or take you to the nearest asylum for further testing and evaluation by helping professionals who only seek to help.

But now, I think my mind is tired, so I am closing my journal entry for today.

## Tuesday, June 12, 2001

New day, new dawn. Is it really Tuesday, it feels like Monday or Wednesday, but when you are out of work it is easy to confuse the days of the week. The only days I can keep straight are the weekend days, Saturday, the Jewish day of rest and Sunday, the Christian day of rest. But Saturday and Sunday are not really rest stays since everybody runs around on those days, goes to stores on those days, goes visiting on those days, even some who work on those days, mostly in retail stores that sell shoddy items made in various Third World sweatshops that use and abuse women and children.

Losing track of days may not be so bad, not really. Think about it. Did God, or if you don't believe in God, did Nature or did any force or forces make the days of the week or even real time for that matter? Not to me, maybe to you, never to me, myself, I. It is all form to me, this clock defined existence, all a way of carving the unending to a final ending and of controlling the human race, confining them or it into definite boxes. Put men in a box and then classify men and then slap yourself on the back for doing so. Hurray. You have achieved something. What have you achieved? Putting people in boxes, classification schemes, beginning with time schemes. What is real and what is unreal. 12:00 p.m., real or unreal. What is real is the rising and setting of the sun, darkness and light, sun and cloudy-ness, rain and heat, cold and snow, real, tangible things in life. The time thing, this month, date thing, just some lines on paper and I don't know why except that everybody wants to make progress, to move somewhere in time, a human instinct or an intellectual instinct of the human brain. I mean, everybody wants to see and measure progression, progression from 10:00 a.m. to 10:00 p.m., moving along, your life moving along in hourly segments, measuring the movement that is we humans. But what would happen if we didn't. Could we still measure things? Measure ourselves? Measure our progress or lack thereof? This presents an interesting question that must be answered by more interesting men and women and not by me, one of the few unemployed workers of American society living in the twenty-first century or thereabouts.

When I think about time, I feel pangs of resentment coming through me or at least pushing through my veins and arteries that are located throughout my body and are components - I think - of my circulatory system. Resentment against employers for using time to destroy everyone that works for them. Time limits, time deadlines, 9 to 5, get in, get working, 12 to 1 lunch time, 5 quitting time, numbers in time; growing up and in school, there was time, 9 to 3, time, periods, art, music, social studies by time, math by time, reading by time, scheduled in days in time segments. Everything in time, scheduling death by time. All of this seems so foolish and stupid and controlling. Why? What reason? Is it again a human need to show progression? I can't fathom that. Maybe it goes back to the Locke and Rousseau thing, the philosophers of the past and present who viewed human beings are freaking fools who didn't know their asses from their elbows and needed some real guidelines to lead them to the true path of virtue. Put humans in time cages, cages like animals, cages used for wild beasts, time cages, and then you can contain their immoral, uncivilized behavior, people's behavior, that is.

Well to hell with that theory, to hell with the Rousseau's and the Locke's and their social contracts and their beliefs in collective representations. To hell with them and to the society built around them, the time/date stamp society built around them. These nitwits, French and English or whatever they were, worked off of one horrible, moronic predisposition, or disposition to be disposed or despised. Men are not beasts, nor are beasts really beasts for that matter. I have come into contact with many individuals in my day and observed many more and I wish to inform you, or at least direct this thought to you, that men are good, down-deep most of us try to always do the right thing, try is the operative term. Animals, well, yes humans are animals, but in the good sense. I like animals, don't you? What I do not like, I mean, in terms of individuals that is, are those I might term as institutional individuals, those representing institutions who talk for institutions, company's, corporations, governments, who talk for the power elite. So what the heck am I talking about now! Well, let me put it to you simply: I have rarely if ever been cheated by an ordinary individual whether in ordinary life or in ordinary business dealings; however, I have been cheated by not-so-ordinary individuals representing big companies, big governments, and big institutions (including hospitals, law firms, insurance companies, universities, etc., etc., etc.). Humans are good, but put them into something big, into structures and something goes terribly wrong.

And the wrong you see now all around you and the wrong you saw all around you in the shape and form of history, is not the ordinary man's fault, or the ordinary woman's fault, it is the fault of men and women, maybe even children, representing the big and the powerful, governments, kings and queens, and men of wealth and reputation who control half the world, and powerful religious jokers in their powerful religious edifices where false piety is parceled out on paper plates.

My final word and thought of this day then: HUMAN BEINGS ARE INTRINSICALLY GOOD. If anybody tells you differently, they are either fools or liars and if they are liars, they represent the power elite as we now know it and should be castigated and downgraded to a place outside your main circle of interests.

### Wednesday, June 13, 2001

So today, I actually got out of the house for a short time, one of my first outings since unemployment came on to me. Maybe I have been depressed, maybe, and that's why I have not left the house, or maybe a bigger maybe is that there has been no place for me to go in the suburbs. What is there except cookie cutter streets, deserted houses, occasional schools, strip malls along the main roads, highways running diagonally and leading to open fields and open concrete shopping malls offering pre-packaged goods, pre-packaged in some vacant lots in Indonesia or somewhere just as ridiculous. But I forced myself, to go into this world, world of suburban dyslexia because this would be good for me, like medicine. What would I do in the house but wait for Headhunters to call me, which they never did. Sitting by the phone and waiting for the next job opportunity or job offer which was never an opportunity and never a good job offer, which instead was always a jail sentence of sorts, why? Go out, be a man, enjoy the world that men have made, go ahead, Cyrus, go, move.

So there I have into the world, taking the four cylinder car on the well-paved roads and to the highway and beyond. As the car moves and I with it, I get a bad feeling in the pit of my stomach, a feeling that doesn't exactly tell me to turn back, but one that instead questions why I am continuing the journey. Where am I going anyway? Why would I want to go anyway? The only purpose for going is to buy, so I guess I will have to buy things, to spend money as an American, giving the money to Americans in exchange for un-American goods. The whole thing bores me but what is the alternative, the walls of the house, interior rooms, hitting buttons at the computer, hitting buttons on the television, watching images that bear no reality to reality, listening to radios with airwaves cluttered with indecipherable sounds of indecipherable people; reading books, books about humans when I no longer like humans, reading about them and their lives, why? Continuing on the road, directing the car, I, until finally hitting one of the great monoliths of modern society, the mall, a complex of buildings, attached and unattached, mostly made of gray concrete and surrounded on all sides by tar roads inside of which are parking lots that stretch as far as the eye can see. And there are cars everywhere. So this is where humanity hangs its hat. Fascinating. I have found the source.

Parking the car someplace, anyplace in the massive parking lot of lots of cars, heading towards buildings, many buildings, looking for entrances and always fearful of forgetting where I parked. In the suburbs, losing your car in the vastness of the malls is a concern. It can happen easily and you can spent the greater portion of the rest of your life searching, which might be good in a spiritual sense but never in a physical sense where food and adequate shelter as an aid against the elements is naturally required. How often have I lost my car in the vastness and ran up and down, back and forward, humans few and far between, passing you while you are frantic, mostly families, or single women, or women in packs, passing while you are in a panic. There is nobody to call, to contact. Where is the local police station? Where is the nearest cop? Where is humanity to lend a human to help? So I worry and try to mark where I have parked my car, mark it in my memory and attempting to place the car within landmarks, where no landmarks exist.

Inside, finally, inside the buildings of the mall, inside and walking on the Italian marble malls and the fancy mirrors and limestone staircases, and more polished marbles and stores lining the walls, stores selling buttons, expensive dresses, children's clothing, infant's clothing, wigs, expensive but bad paintings and art prints, books that are the most current and the most inane, toys that are the most current and the most inane, bathroom gadgets that are unnecessary, kitchen gadgets that are unnecessary, hand-blown glass curiosities, ribbons, bows, bangles, greeting cards, sports cards, etc., etc., etc. On and on stores on three, five, ten levels, stores offering different merchandise but all the same merchandise, boring stores, stores that smell of recent disinfectant, stores with teenage workers, high school and college kids who have no idea about their future or anybody's future, the world's future, or, even what the future means. You go in and ask the kids a question about the merchandise and they look perplexed; after a time, you stop asking the questions. The stores themselves, the names, inconsequential, 'Cathy's Place', 'Place of Hair', 'Kids Corner,' 'DDs,' etc., etc., and more and more etc. These are all chain stores or franchise stores - who the hell knows the difference - and you can tell they are chain or franchise stores because in every mall you go to, they are there, these stores, with the same young kids manning the aisles and cash registers and with the same sanitary smells. You can go into one mall and not be able to tell which of the many malls it is. Inside it is the same, nothing to distinguish it. In the most modern sense, this might be good, at least to some with half and sometimes a quarter of a peanut-sized brain. And the reason it is good - to those with the miniscule brains - is that you can mix and match everything, you can buy from one store in one mall and return it to the same store in another mall (exchange is the word) and there you go. They also like it because they always know what to expect when they go into a mall, what stores there will be, what sales their will be, etc. and on and on. They do not like surprises, to be surprised, or have the surprise be on them. It is a stable, controlled world with little discomfort anywhere in sight.

Mass production, Henry Ford and the Assembly Line, this is the outcome, the modern mall with the thousands of items that all lead to one. Mass production for the masses, items all the same for different people that are all the same in malls that are all different but all the same, malls created on assembly lines that are all the same. Sameness, humans being fit into the pattern of sameness on the assembly line of life masquerading as life and death. Walking the marbled floor of the mall, and watching the people during the day, the weekday, and there are mostly women here, housewives they used to call them, pushing baby-carriages in pairs or in threes or fours, with little kids tailing them at their ankles, little kids and women everywhere, young single women also, with dizzying looks, analyzing store windows, with bags in hand, treasures collected at the mall. There is an occasionally man, looking slightly perplexed, maybe on vacation; he is wearing casual clothing, meaning not a shirt and tie for business but casual slacks and shirts and sneakers for real life; but, you can't go buy that anymore since businesses now allow many employees to go casual, which is good and bad. Let the worker feel comfortable is the motto, but my motto is, let the worker be comfortable so you can get more out of the worker, drain him to the last drop but make him feel comfortable while doing so. Makes sense to me. It is like giving somebody rope or more rope to hang themselves. Makes sense to me. Manipulation to the utmost.

I sit along a marble ledge along this enclosed centerpiece area, behind which are plantings of huge Ficus trees and huge Dracaena trees that are maintained by some external landscaping place hired by the mall. This greenery is supposed to provide the customers with that sense of the outdoors and that sense of nature that is absent from the man-made concrete walls around them.

Failure, this is a failure, a failing effort, or, something of an abomination to life as lived in our lives. Let's put it like this, to take a fine, rare diamond and display it in the middle of a pig pen with mud and grime and smells everywhere, does this do justice to the diamond; does the diamond raise the pig pen to the status of a world class palace of animal husbandry? Of course not. The diamond somehow loses its luster and becomes another tarnished piece of debris. Sitting here, balancing on the ledge observing the booth next to me where two young blondes in red and black business suits are selling mobile phones and various other electronic gadgets that are not worthy of particular mention. Everybody who passes their booth, short or tall, black or white, male or female, they stop, give them these handouts and deliver this pitch about joining up with their service. "And you will get a phone at cost and 200 minutes every month of unlimited calling during the week and 60 minutes on weekends, and. . . ." Most just keep walking, taking the handouts and walking and walking and dumping the handouts in the nearest plastic garbage bin. A few stay - mostly the guys - to listen to the young blondes deliver their spiels in sexy voices that remind of sexual things like fervid intercourse during the heat of a July afternoon. Of these who stay to listen, one in five buy; the rest, they move on after getting their share of flirtation coitus interruptus. After a time I get bored with this and wander over into what is termed, 'Candy Time,' a place selling loose candies out of glass trays. The procedure is to take a plastic bag and help yourself to the candy of your choice. My choice is the sugar-free malt balls, a favorite of mine ever since I started having favorites. I then take the bag to the counter and to the only employee of 'Candy Time' then in the store, a young high school age lad with freckles, a little overweight and with a twitch in one eye. He takes my bag and puts it on a scale. "That will be fourteen dollars, Sir," the lad announces without a laugh or whimper. "What?" question I. "How can that be? Fourteen dollars for a bag of candy?" The lad looks confused. "Sir, the sign on the wall over their clearly states that all candy is twelve dollars a pound and you have purchased a little more than a pound." I look at the sign he is point to, a little placard along a back wall with print that isn't large enough to fit in the eye of a needle. "Do you still want the candy sir?" I leave the candy and walk away from 'Candy Time' and keep walking out of the enclosed mall.

Adjacent to the main mall, within the parking lot complex are a couple of fast food burger joints and a large hardware store that is part of a huge chain stretching nationwide, worldwide, to the ends of the world, and soon coming to Mars, Jupiter, Venus, and Saturn if it ever warms up. I stroll over to the great hardware store and venture inside. Why? Nothing better to do except to go home to the walls, and to the enclosure that holds the walls. Anyway, I have grown to like wandering through this chain store, I have grown to enjoy examining the wrenches, looking at the lumber, remonstrating over the houseplants and outdoor plants, eyeing the electric bulbs and electric sockets, and all the various things created to improve or fix the home for the homeowner. Up and down the aisles I go, looking at the customers - mostly men, many of whom are construction contractors pushing wagon-loads of heavy lumber - and wondering what they were going to do with their purchases and wishing I could be more like them. I don't like home repair, or, even repairing the home. I know nothing about it, don't want to know anything about it, always pay somebody else to know something about it and pay somebody to do it. The only thing that I know about is houseplants and growing them in my basement, in my backyard, potting and repotting and replanting, I know this. Putting up a ceiling fan, I do not know about, re-wiring the kitchen, I do not know about, remodeling the attack, I certainly do not know about and the list goes on. So why am I wandering the aisles of a home repair/hardware store. It is the male in me, I guess, and my love of gadgets and imagining their possibilities and imagining myself using them sometime in the future when I become interested in home repairs. Of course, this makes no sense, but does anything make sense.

After an hour or two wandering the aisles, I make my way out of the store, find my car and head home where I anticipate having mail in the mailbox from potential employers and phone messages on the answering phone from potential employers. When I get home, there are no potential employers anyway in site. Thus, my day ends, or, at least terminates at this point.


## Thursday, June 14, 2001

At my computer, a lot now; where else does one head in a house abandoned by the world to an unemployed adult way past the age of infancy. What else is there to do here? Sit in front of the television and scroll through all the channels, which come to nothing anyway. People talking or explaining or showing, others lecturing; movies of humans trying to find answers, movies of humans trying to be funny or sad, what does it come to. Sports on the television set can be okay, but there are little live sports during the day when people are at work. There are the countless sports-highlight shows that grow lame after awhile and boring and other such things. I mean, once you hear the scores what else can there be, once you know the final results, what else can there be. Right? Wrong? Knowing the final score is almost like knowing exactly when you are going to die. Having the box score is like having information on what you will die of. You really do not want to know that most of the time. Yeah, you can watch the television and view the sports highlights and sports events when they are on during the day, but in the end, even for the avid sports fan, it becomes boring, mundane, old hat, year after year, the same games, the same goals, the same monotony. World Series, Super Bowl, Stanley Cup, etc., etc., etc. titles, win and celebrations and do it again next year, forget this year, do it next year. Sports like business, what have you done for me lately; it is a depressing thing and in the end, makes you doubt the reality of what is.

Bored with television and the information it provides, countless words providing supposed entertainment or supposed information and in the end, you can't remember any of it. It is like dead air in dead space. It is like that with the mass media, which is really mass. You take it in, television shows, movies, radio, newspapers, you take them all in, squeeze out what you want, retain little or retain for a second and then it is all gone. Retaining for a second is something quite interesting. Like you can retain a movie for a second or so, or, even a good book for a second or so and we can classify most popular books these days - mass produced in mass production factories for the masses - in this category, and music recordings (albums) in this category. Retaining for the moment, word of mouth for the moment being promulgated for the moment, movies, television programs, books, records, ideas within them retained for a second or two and this retention is used and worked upon to sell more; the class at the top, selling to the class at the bottom that retention, using word of mouth about that retention, retention of something from the movie or television show and making money off the retention. But the retention is usually minimal and when it has served its purpose, it too, that little spark will disappear, flicker out, usually unless there is some more profit involved, and so it will be retained. And thus, we have the birth of the 'classic,' or, in real terms the birth of the perpetual money maker, AKA, the Beatles hits or Dickens' works or William Shakespeare's greatest hits, yes, perpetual glories to bask in, to make money on, to retain, a few thoughts that are passing to retain.

All of this does make me flinch because I am no Marxist and whenever I make some economic argument I feel like one for whatever reason imaginable. I mean Marx had his point, Lenin had his points but so did Adam Smith and other capitalist men of past grandeur. The simplistic, that is something I dislike, Marx as simplistic, Adam Smith and philosophies of capitalism - simplistic. It isn't that simplistic or that complex. You cannot put human motivation down to one factor or two factors. Simplification is for simpletons; all you do by simplifying is create unbearable simple situations that lead to twentieth centuries filled with violence and exploitation and various calamities too terrible to mention within this sentence. So let me conclude, simplistic solutions and philosophies are too simplistic and lift isn't too complex either, but the minute you treat things simplistically, watch out for the fireworks below.

Life isn't simple, but it is deep, has depth, has multitudes of thoughts and patterns chunked up within in, pushed deep into it from an individual's childhood and that makes it varied and interesting and keeps us all from being equal, which is good. We don't want carbon-copies to be produced from the assembly lines of fourth rate nations around the globe. So while simplistic is not good, depth of experiences is definitely good. And by experiences and depth in life, we are talking about every waking moment of every waking day that one exists on this planet, meetings with humans and animals and plants; sickness, health, tragedies, funerals, births, deaths, all experiences like hairs on the head of a once bald man. Hairs building up until the there is so much on the cranium that the hippie would be in awe.

A day, in the home, at the computer, not at the television set. My mind is blank now, can't go on with this now. I have a headache. I must lie down, close my eyes and try to forget my own isolation. That is my only choice.

### Friday, June 15, 2001

Bad day, that previous day, filled with undefined depression, but luckily for me it just lasted the day; I am not want to go into precipitous declines. They are short and sweet, the mental declines that is, and I am able to come out of the pit quickly. There are others, friends I have known and not know, who cannot rise, who face life and are flattened by it and then must see professional men of all stripes who provide them with pills and more pills like a candy man providing children with jawbreakers; only then can they rise up after months, years, only then with artificial substances in their intestines can they rise but only briefly because they will fall back, sadly fall to the ground and need other professional men with other substances that are not natural in pill form to pop into their mouths.

I am lucky then, or crazy then, because I can fall and then rise from day to day, be down and then up like the stock market, and today I am up or at least level and I can sit at my computer and play with its shiny buttons. I hit the buttons and it takes me to blue and red and green screens, it takes me to the Internet where I can interact with the world, a world I don't really want to interact with for reasons I have previously stated but can hear re-state. Who wants to be connected to the world? Plugged in! Tuned in! What does the world have to offer except a very human connection and with that connection news of mans inhumanity to man and mans trying to sell to men. Internet, a selling device, or a device that shows us as a race to be inane as a race. Plugging in instead of unplugging completely. But if you unplug completely you will be classified as some social misfit, an intellectual deviate, a morale deviate, an anti-social deviate, onwards and upwards. Lock out the world and they tell you, you are locking out humanity and that there is something wrong with that. Something wrong with what? Why should there be something wrong with putting the ways of man off in some corner and existing on your plane. But I have said that already to everyone so I do not want to repeat myself.

The buttons, connecting, back to the computer and the Internet. The Internet generation, computers everywhere, another revolution following the industrial revolution, following mass manufacturing techniques, assembly lines, factories, sweatshops, exploitation of natural resources and workers, another revolution, technology. Another crock. What were some of the previous revolutions, agrarian revolution, green revolution, republican revolution, scientific revolution? What has all that come to and what will come of it. Push buttons, get responses across a digital divide; unite Africa and America in one fell swoop. Cruising along, me alone in the house, family separate by space and time and me cruising along on the Internet, going from page to page, searching for information that will provide some answers to why I am here on this planet. And that is a common thread, searching for the reason, which the social scientists call the meaning of life, searching for it. Going on to the computer, a device with circuit boards and wires and silicon chips and metal and glue and whatever else, punching the buttons and expecting meaning; sometimes, occasionally, not expecting anything and not receiving anything. Do most people expect meaning through pressing of buttons that land them on top of the electronic highway? A good question. Meaning, maybe they don't think about it, but instinctively, they are looking for a reason to live, that is, to pass the time, to make time go, to eat that time. In a funny way, our diversions and our methods are ways of us finding meaning. The meaning of life becomes the diversion of life. Playing volleyball on the beach with strangers is the diversion and the meaning. Going to dinner at a fine restaurant is the diversion and the meaning. The meaning can be the diversion and the diversion can be the meaning. Some might be the choice of diversions, shallow and the person choosing diversions to be shallow, but who is to say, who is to judge. To find meaning in life, what is the meaning in life? Is helping other human beings the meaning in life. Who said? Did some bible say that, some philosopher's quill? Meaning is whatever you want the meaning to be.

One of my problems in life is this idea of meaning. I have always looked for it and never found it and certainly being unemployed doesn't help this helpless feeling I feel down in my very little soul. I wonder about others and if they have found meaning. These others, I don't care what the world says about them, that they have found meaning, a great scientist or doctor or lawyer or writer, etc., etc., etc., if the world says they found meaning, or if the world says the family man has found meaning. Have they really. What about those who seem to have found meaning, the successes, the humanitarians, who commit suicide and nobody seems to know why? Did they really find meaning? I am of the opinion that maybe meaning cannot be found, be found on the Internet or in books, or in religion, or in family and friends, that meaning really is diversion and diversion is actually meaning.

The thoughts are depressing me again. Random access thoughts for the random access computer. Thank God, it's Friday again and I will soon have my family for the weekend again, thank God.

# WEEK 3

## Monday, June 18, 2001

Today I am into the unemployment thing and in it real deep. I have the Want Ads in my hand from yesterday's paper and have circled all these bullshit jobs and there I am, there you have it, me, sitting down, finding ads, circling ads, and there will be resumes to send out. I do it, at first with glee, then with less glee, and then with a sick feeling in the pit of my stomach. I circle about ten job ads and am will email my resumes to the prospective employers or the prospective headhunting firms hired by the prospective employers. It's easy to send resumes this way; just press a button here and a button there on the computer and you can send out hundreds within a half second or less; you can send your resume to everyone existing on this planet in a second and one half, that is, if everyone existing on this planet has a computer, or access to one, which of course they don't, God forbid. But sick I get in reading and circling the ads and then emailing them. The words that they always use: BRIGHT, SELF-STARTER, METICULOUS, EXPERIENCED, KNOWLEDGE OF THIS TECHNOLOGY OR THAT TECHNOLOGY, ABLE TO MEET DEADLINES, ABLE TO WORK WELL WITH OTHERS, UNDERSTANDS FINANCIAL CONCEPTS, UNDERSTANDS MEDICAL CONCEPTS, UNDERSTANDS INSURANCE CONCEPTS, UNDERSTANDS REAL ESTATE CONCEPTS, UNDERSTANDS LEGAL CONCEPTS. Sick, the words, the verbiage thrown like thunder under a bridge. How dare they, how dare they ask for this and that, demand I meet their deadlines and the like. The real question is: will they meet my deadlines, my real question is do they work well with employees, my real question is do they understand that basic concepts of humanity and decency? I always get a kick when the ads offer a great benefit package or a great medical package or vacation package. How often does that mean they don't pay, that is the salary is not enough to support a nest of frogs sitting on their tadpoles in the middle of a cold Vermont winter. They are always vague about these benefits in their ads anyway and usually when you find out the real truth, the truth is not so nice. When they offer a great vacation package that means you can have a day of vacation after your first ten years of consecutive employment. The catch is you will never reach that tenth year; you will be out the door before that happens. Cynical in approach, but I have learned the cynicism. Pension, offering great retirement benefits, but again there is the grandfather clause, benefits accruing only after years of service, but you will be disposed of long before that point. They are no fools; you are the fool for accepting their fools gold. Self Starter, that means they want to just hand a worker jerk a load of responsibility and then walk away; in other words, they do not want to do their job of teaching and supervising. They want you to do their job and your job; they want you to have your ass on the line, not their ass on the line. That's what they want from their employee, that's what they are looking for in their job advertisement. The common Joe, he generally has few rights as an employee. He is at the mercy of others, the higher ups, who can use and abuse and then dispose. That is what I see in these job advertisements, the little man getting smaller and smaller, use and abuse until death do us part.

Monday, God, I feel so sick. I wish my children were home, my son were home and it was the weekend, and we'd be in the front throwing the ball around. He's eleven now and a friend with a spirit. Being with him, it makes me forget. My daughter, eight, tender, beautiful, being with her, playing with her, eating meals with her and my son, listening to my wife's voice yelling orders at all of us, makes me forget the hell of the work world and the unemployment world. It is hard to bear.

### Tuesday, June 19, 2001

Unemployment daydreams washed away briefly by knowledge that the summer is coming, that my son is graduating elementary school, that my daughter is graduating second grade and that my wife's teaching year is about to end. Of course, all of this is obliterated in my mind's eye by the fact that my wife will be teaching summer school due to my current circumstances and the fact that there are real bills that need to be paid, and the fact that my son will be going away to sleep-a-way camp for a month as soon as his school ends, and that my daughter will be going to day camp for the summer. I will be alone again of course, unless I find a job, which is highly unlikely now. The economy has gone into the toilet and the technology side of the economy is even worse and I'm in that technology side being a technical writer, a writer of boring technical material hired out by technical corporations which are not technical in any sense except that they technically know how to make technical money. I have a friend who told me of the downturn, that's what they call depressions now, told me that jobs were impossible to come by, that many companies had gone belly up. I am caught in it, in the swirl, being pulled under by a lack of opportunity, which isn't opportunity anyway, which is really prison anyway. How much luck is involved in life then, depression, downturn, upturns, wealth, success, everything going in cycles and you can only hope you are there at a good cycle and not a bad cycle. Luck of the draw or luck of the Irish. I have no luck. There is no hope in cycle only down cycles.

The summer coming but I am not coming. The family all busy, the world all busy and I not busy. How can that be? Why am I left out of everything? Why is life speeding by so quickly and I am not with life. Why am I left behind at the station while the train pours forward, the great locomotive that is filled with so much hope and promise but not for me, not for one who is being left behind. But maybe it is all illusion, maybe there is no progress or progression or trains leaving me behind. So what if others do things. It is all illusion anyway. Movement doesn't signify success, nor, does movement signify meaning. Back to the world meaning, again. I hate this, hate my life.

Looking at the world and feeling it is up ahead and you are behind. Is this illusion? Am I behind? Where should I be? Where is it written that I should be ahead, should have money, should be rich, should have money in the bank, should be prepared for retirement. Why do I live my life with such illusions? Lies, all lies. Are these illusions or preconceptions? The preconception is that somebody my age should be financially secure, have a good, solid job, and be secure in his life and knowing about his life in general. That is the preconception. Stupid. The reality is how many of us know anything about anything. Even those who know, do not know. You plan, you do, and then you die of cancer or heart disease or get run over by a bus. How many get a beautiful wife/husband with the best looking kids and then wind up in middle age divorced and on the street looking in. Ideas of how we should be, where we should be serve no purpose except to drive us nuts and make us unhappy. The only preconception we should have is to have a conception of life; to keep breathing, day after day, that should be the conception, preconception, that should be the illusion and the delusion. I have spoken!

### Wednesday, June 20, 2001

Wednesday in isolation or is it isolation on Wednesday. One doesn't have anything to do with the other, at least, I don't think so. What do I mean by that? There is nothing special about a Wednesday that puts people in an isolated state. The days of the week, however, definitely have an effect on humans, however, even if the days of the week are artificial elements created by those humans. How often, when I was working at a job of not my choosing, did I see my co-workers downbeat on a Monday

morning? Depressed, upset, knowing that they had a whole week
at their rotten job. I never was depressed on Monday morning;
the reason I was just too nervous. Monday morning the bosses'
always are busy trying to justify their inflated paychecks and as a
consequence they yell out demands and orders and deadlines to
their staff - the common working stiff - and as a consequence
there is incredible tension and as a consequence many people
begin developing heart disease and other fatal diseases without
knowing it. My policy on Monday morning on any job was
always to hide underneath the desk, let the bosses not see me, let
few people see me until the storm of Monday morning passed
over me. Thus, Monday was never a bad day for me in terms of
my mental state. I was always into the job on Monday morning,
finding ways to hide from the powers that be that will always be
powers until a Board of Directors ask them to leave for being too
powerful. Tuesdays were the bad days, knowing that I had gotten
through Monday, hidden successfully, and now had the whole
rest of the work week to deal with. Horrible. Wednesday, not a
bad day; sometimes I'd call in sick on Wednesday, because it cut
the work week in half and after coming back on Thursday there
was only two work days left. Thursday, somewhat like Tuesday
but with light at the end of the tunnel. I could see the weekend
coming. Friday, a day to relax, do as little as work as possible,
anticipate the weekend and what I was going to do on the
weekend. Many of the people I worked with, the common dude I
am speaking of here, felt the same way about the working days of
the week. There were variations on themes of course, what with
vacations and religious and national holidays to break the
monotony of work and for most of us, it is the monotony that was
the worst, although anticipation of the boss yelling at you or
manipulating you or ignoring you did not make you happy either.
To me, the monotony of the job, most white collar jobs that is,
office jobs, within lifeless and colorless buildings, on floors that
are lifeless and colorless, glass, metal, gray cubicles, grayer
office equipment, sitting there in front of terminals at a desk,
pencil, paper, phone, every day the same, the same people with
the same problems, doing the same paperwork, facing the same
boredom; the whole thing is like being in jail in some far away

prison that they make movies about. But I have to make this conditional. Some of my co-workers, drones like myself, always can get into their drone-work, and they do this by pretending that their drone work is very important drone work, important to the financial future of the corporation, important to the financial future of their country and maybe of the world. They see themselves as vital in the entire process. Every time they place numbers in a spreadsheet or a database or type a letter on the computer or answer a customers nonsensical question on the telephone, they view themselves as doing a great deed, akin to the greatest humanitarian act. They deluded themselves, really, and the delusion always ends for them when that great corporation in the sky lays them off or fires them and then puts another body in their place that functions just as well as they. Thus, they weren't needed after all. Nobody needs them. They will come to terms with this fact until they get their next job when they will once again delude themselves on some level about their own importance. But there are still others, the drone workers, who are under no such illusions, but who deal with the monotony of the most common office job by bullshitting all day, walking about, talking with co-workers about sports or public events, or, politics or religion, making jokes, telling jokes, listening to jokes, commenting about the bosses, commenting about other co-workers, and thus, they get through the boredom and thus they earn their paycheck. Isn't it wonderful? Another variation of theme these days are worker drones who play at their computers all day when the bosses are not looking; they play card games and they play on the Internet, shopping at auctions or just searching for the merchandise offered, or going to the news pages or sports pages, hitting keys and surfing the net, that's it, all day until the end of the working day when they are released.

This is all fine until you think about it. Our lives are finite. So wasting time in an office as a white collar worker of the world is not the thing to do. Each second that becomes a waste product, represents a passel of brain cells from your body that die forever. It is a sad state of affairs that can drive you nuts when you think about it, and which drives me nuts when I always think about it. Lucky for most people who inhabit the white collar neighborhoods of work-dom, they never think about it.


### Thursday, June 21, 2001

Continuing on the theme of yesterday, the meaninglessness of white collar work and the white collar workload, and the boredom and the monotony encountered, I have a related theme, a theme which derives from my last job at a small, but growing company that manufactured financial software for the computer, software that was and is used by financial people in the major markets of the world to make more money than they are already making. The theme here is called the business plan; that is the term that this employer used with his subjects (the working rabble). To 'Grow A Business' you need a 'Business Plan.' That is what was being continuously said around the halls of the byways and tri-ways of my ex-employer and at first I had difficulty understanding the lingo. I watched as the employer (now with the ex- attached to it), kept hiring more and more employees, more and more when there was no need for more and more and no money from the profits of the company for more and more. So why hire? To grow the business for the business plan. Listening to it, not understanding it. It didn't make sense to me, especially when I would see the new workers at their desks ready for work but not receiving any. What was going on? This was not logical? Investigating further and it is discovered that the company - in its five years of life - never turned a profit. How could that be? Profits no. Growing the business, yes. Business plan, yes. Strange world and reading the newspapers I kept seeing all these new words, or, at least new words to me.

Well, I have learned the terms, the byways and bylaws and sophisticated corporate blabber and the blarney and all the rest that comes with making big money in this day and age and it all comes down to marketing and stocks and bonds and doing things like going public, which means taking a private company and making it a public company buy selling stock shares to the highest bidders and stock prices going up and insiders trading the new shares and insiders selling their new shares and insiders walking away with tidy profits on their sold shares. They call this process with the stocks IPO which means Initial Public Offering or something like that and most of the employees in the place don't know crap about this but hear the terms and know that their employer might be offering stock options, which means that they get options to buy the stock when the company first goes public, and buy the stock at the lowest prices, or, something like that. But very few of the workers really do understand. Their interest is mostly in continuing to bring home a paycheck, to pay the mortgage, and the gas and electric bills, to buy food for them and their kids, to buy clothing, to plan the one week vacation to an amusement park somewhere and mostly, just to hold their heads above water. So what does stock options, growing a business, public and private offerings and all this other bullshit mean to them? To them it isn't real, something they could touch. To them, the common working stiff - and I am included in the bunch of stiffs - they understand the concrete and nothing that sounds too theoretical.

Fine, okay, now what about the business plan thing, where does that fit into the whole crock of waste products? Kind of, sort of, figured it out, slightly, not surely, figured, got some idea. It fits in with the profit thing and the lack thereof. When you don't turn a profit, you have to get money from somewhere, and where is the somewhere? From people, from other businesses, investors they call them collectively and to get people, other businesses, investors you have to show them things on paper and what you show them on paper has to make them happy. And if they become happy it is because they figure that this private company is going to become a public company then and that its stock will be bought and sold and they will get that stock at the lowest prices and turn around and sell it at the highest prices. Presto, instant cash, instant profit. Boy that was easy. But to make this whole crazy scheme take off, you got to have that business plan, that thing on paper that looks great to the investor who isn't on paper and who has that ready cash on hand. And as part of the business plan, you have to have all the monkeys, that is, your employers in place, and these employees have to have the right titles, because investors look for these right titles, so you have to go out there and hire financial analysts and computer programmers and project managers and business analysts, quality assurance analysts, customer service personnel, etc., etc., etc. And there you have it. When potential money-pocketed people come into the company to decide whether to invest their easy-gotten money into the business, they look at the bodies and they analyze the paper business plan. Thus, we have it or I have it, but never really wanted it.

There are always variations to these things, many of which I have no understanding of and which I really don't want an understanding of. The bottom line for me is that this is a different world that I am existing in, a different world of business than I am used to. To me a business used to mean, producing a fathomable product and selling it at a profit, making profits, hiring people from those profits, building the business from those profits and then turning out more products with the process continuing from there. But that's not it completely anymore, as I have learned from this last job and the job before that. Pre-conceptions have been dashed. Complicated rituals have sprung up, complicated concepts and perambulations have sprung up. I am a babe in the woods and there are hungry bears all around.

I am lost and I freely admit to it.

### Friday, June 22, 2001

Interesting entry in this journal since it is not the usual day of unemployment for me. Late this morning I am to attend my son's graduation from elementary school. My wife is teaching today but meeting me at the graduation. My son went to school, however, and my daughter is there, so I have a few hours to kill before the time arrives.

Graduation, his elementary school, combined with my unemployment, is an interesting combination in my mind. I am reminded of my own elementary school days, the halls of the school, the lunch room, the teachers, the feelings of dread and maybe of promise. I should be glad on this day but all I can think of is where it went wrong. Was there something I could have done differently as a kid? Should I have studied harder? Been a better student? Been a better athlete? Been a better son? Followed religion more? Been a friendlier person and had more friends? How does my unemployment now come as a result of my elementary school years? Well, there is a connection, there always is a connection in life, an individual's life that is. We are - now I swear this is true - just a combination of experiences combined with genetic factors and all that sort of rot. And each moment of our lives is chained together with all other moments. So, there, proof that what I did in elementary school is related and possibly the cause of my current case of unemployment du jour.

But this is indicating that being unemployed is somehow a horrible thing or a sign of a lack of something or a lack of character, or that being unemployed is some sort of shame. That is what I am implying in this whole thing. Why should I be analyzing my life to try to understand the unemployment situation anyway? Why would I go back to my elementary days to try to understand them to understand my present state of being without a paycheck? Does it make sense? Well, maybe, if I keep thinking about it. Maybe if when I was a kid, I had applied myself a little more - which I definitely did not - things would have been better for me. If I had somehow been wiser when I was eleven, if I had made up my mind to study, to become a doctor or a lawyer, or engineer, or, any sort of professional man then, I wouldn't be having such trouble now, would I be having such trouble now? Professionals, real ones, the doctor, the plumber, the electrician, do not have the troubles I have had in my so called career, going from job to job, corporation to corporation, accumulating nothing, gaining nothing. If I had become a doctor, there would have been one or two jobs, big money, my own office, a fancy house and cars, trips, etc., etc. If I had chosen another profession, there would have been success, less worry, stability, more material joys, etc., etc., etc. It goes back to elementary school, doesn't it, the lack of direction that is. But who is to blame for that, a ten year old boy or, or, or, his parents.

Can we blame my parents, or anybody's parents for their child growing up unemployed and unemployable? Should the parents have provided more direction? What if the parents are uneducated themselves, have no ideas either, and are often unemployed themselves, what kind of guidance can they give? What type of guidance can any parent give? I have no idea nor do I really care to have an idea.

The idea of blaming parents, the thought, it disgusts me. If you blame parents, that means you cannot blame yourself and if you do that, you are a fool, at least to me. I like the individual approach, an individual is responsible to his/her individual self. The universe is the individual, the individual is the universe. Now there is my concept. And while we are at it, while we discuss the blame thing, I would like to cast my vote against blaming poverty or lack of opportunity or luck or God as the culprit in my current predicament. God did not cause my unemployment, neither did my lower middle class upbringing. I envy nobody for having grown up better, with that silver spoon. Too much time is wasted on envy. In the end, it all comes back to you and me and responsibility for ourselves. The world is ours; we make it ours; it is nobody else's; that's it.

So there we go, around and around, but I should be happy today, today my son is graduating elementary school, which means I am growing older and closer to death. There I go again, down and downcast, a person who looks at the downside. I cannot help myself. The world looks dark to me, even in the happiest of times. As long as death exists on this planet, I will be down and dark.

I'm rambling. I must stop this. I must get hold of myself. I have to leave. The graduation is in less than an hour and I must put on a happy face. The world deserves a happy face on happy occasions.

# WEEK 4

## Monday, June 25, 2001

Graduation, you remember me mentioning it, followed by a weekend. The graduation, children dressed up, saluting flags, civic associations giving speeches, Principal and teachers giving speeches, making generalized pronouncements which mean nothing, official speeches of official people who paint the future as one of hope and opportunity for young people My question, how can their be hope and opportunity for young people when young people turn into older people and older people are generally sons of a bitches who destroy all they touch, pervert all they touch, rip the petals off the prettiest flowers. That is the world of older people that young people will be going into. And the younger people will become the older people soon enough and they will become dirt bags and filth and destroyers of everything around them. Perversity everywhere but not at the elementary school graduation where everything smells like perfume and there are beautiful flowering roses on the horizon.

What I particularly hated was watching these overstuffed adults, filled with themselves and their own inanity, get up their on stage and tell us all - parents and parents-parents - how it was up to our young people to build a better world. We should have built that better world centuries ago, don't you think so! Why should be leave it up to our children. We use our children, and that's the truth, we use our young people and that's the bigger truth, in fact, we seduce these young people; use them as fodder for our corrupt corruptions and corrupt governments. We promise them the world, we praise them to the world so they can do our dirty work, run our companies, fight our wars, and once they do, we throw them into the common waste-pile of older people. Abusive systems down through the ages, this is the fact of life. But what to do? How to fight it? You cannot announce this. Nobody will believe it, most will not believe it. Make such announcements and the next thing you know, society has excluded you, your family and friends (if there are any), have excluded you. There it is right there and that is and was my dilemma at my son's graduation. You could see me sitting there, watching the nonsense, clapping at the boring nonsense, sitting and sitting like you doing in churches or synagogues or mosques or temples, sitting and sitting and listening and being bored but pretending interest. All this pretending, it is sick and repellent to the utmost. But again, what can you do? Hide, maybe. Go to Walden's Pond? Maybe. Find a dark cave, bring cans of baked beans and bottled water and live there the rest of your life? Maybe. Maybe but no maybe. I and we are too rational to do that, to break away. I and we are too cowardly to do that, we are too conformist to do that.

How foolish it is, the world, the games, playing games, pretending to go along while you know it is all wrong. Thus, you go along and become part of the problem, a destroyer of the young and a polluter of the universe. How sick is this!

### Tuesday, June 26, 2001

My son is home today and my daughter is home today, school is done. My wife is still at her school, still being the teacher, the leader of the pack; tomorrow is the end of her school term and then she teaches summer school, must teach summer school because I am teaching nothing, working at nothing, earning nothing of any sort or manner. We are taking my son up to sleep-a-way camp tomorrow, five thousand dollars worth of sleep-a-way camp and my daughter she starts day camp, three thousand dollars worth of day camp. So the kids are home with me today - sleeping in their beds right now - but home with me today. Is this good or bad? I am not used to have anybody home with me during the week while I am unemployed, I am used to being alone with the walls and contemplating my situation, looking for solutions that I find impossible to find, worrying about my future which I believe to be bleak and impossible. Now the question becomes for me at least, is it better for my spirits to be alone or is it better for my spirits to be with other people? Good question. To be with my kids, that is good, but I feel lonely still, but not as lonely; to be with my wife, I feel lonely but not terribly. To be with others, to work with others, to have to talk with others, it is the most alienating thing on earth; I can barely hear them speak or follow their words or meaning. To be alone, apart from people, you feel alienated but in a particular sort of way, you feel isolated but in a particular sort of way. You can get used to being alone; you can never get used to being alone in a crowd; you can only get angry and want to destroy the crowd, or get apathetic and bizarre. Being alone with yourself, you have to learn to deal with yourself. Being alone in a crowd, being at work with your co-workers you can never be alone with yourself, that is never allowed for yourself and thus you can lose yourself and then die one thousand deaths.

Being alone, thinking internally, coming up for the answers yourself, even if those answers are common ideas and thoughts that can be read from any book, this is the essence of having an essence, this is the essence of why we're on the planet. Being alone, isolated, to do and think for ourselves, this is pure and pristine and brings me peace. The crowd, people around me, pulls from me, pulls ideas out and doesn't replenish the ideas, doesn't replenish the energy. It is use and abuse with the people around us, use and abuse, which is called society of man and goes by other things like humanity and that sort of nonsense.

My children are arising and are calling out to me, want me to prepare breakfast, want me to take them out to lunch, want me to play ball with them, want me, asking for me, a compliment or not, a merit or not. To be needed in life, is that a blessing or is that a curse. To be wanted at work, a blessing or a curse? To have people dependent upon you, a blessing or a curse? There are many ways to view that. When people need you, that gives you power, power over them. You are the boss, their boss. They ask you what to do. You tell them; they are at your mercy. After awhile, you might start acting like a boss, playing God as the boss, playing the unjust God, being the puppeteer and playing God and ruining lives playing God. It is a responsibility being the boss. And having others dependent, them looking to you that means you are in charge and you are guilty as charged if something happens, you the boss, can have your head chopped off, that is in the real world. At work, the job, the boss who made the decisions often goes free while the workers pay the price for his idiocy. But what the hell. Have to go. I have my duties.

## Wednesday, June 27, 2001

As opposed to the usual diary entry made in the morning, I am making this diary entry in the late afternoon. Early this morning, we placed my daughter on her day camp bus for the first time and then drove my son, suitcases, packages, bottles, precious foodstuffs and all, up to his sleep-away camp in Upstate New York, a three hour journey through outer New York City boroughs, like the Bronx, on rotting roads filled with trucks and pollution debris, filled with bumper to bumper traffic with my son complaining and then barfing all along the route of car sickness and my wife yelling at me all along the route for reasons yet undetermined and me just keeping my mouth shut and wishing I was alone again, not bothered by the human touch.

Sometimes wishing that you are in another place when you are not is actually helpful. For example, I find myself dreaming of far-off places, sunny and sandy beaches while I am in the dentist's chair being drilled to eternity. I purposely let my mind go there, to other worlds, to more pleasant experiences

while facing the unpleasantness of physical pain of all sorts. It
also can work with mental pain as well. During the day, being
unemployed, in the suburbs, facing the walls of sterile rooms
alone in sterility alone, I dream of going on exotic plant
expeditions in Africa, in Madagascar, in Arabia, me there, in the
middle of forests and trees and jungles, me there, with the sweat
pouring from my temples, me there driving a Jeep, me there
talking to the natives, me there, discovering and naming new
species, me there, being cheered as a hero for my many new
discoveries in the field of botany. Yes, I can see myself making a
name for myself and being known to eternity. Dreaming, there is
nothing wrong with it, although employers for one never like
that. But the good thing about dreaming while you are awake is
that it is free and it is a private thing unless you share it. It, the
dreaming allows you to push away what is so unpleasant in life -
people's preoccupation with getting you to do what they want you
to do. In waking dreams, you can be the way you want to be; do
as you like; live as you like; and, be as moral or sadistic as you
like.

Ah, but I hear the dissenters now, those of the psychiatric
and every other helping profession that pretends to help you, I
can hear their yapping traps now, very loud and clear, hearing
their lousy words which are only words of manipulation. What do
they say, these professional manipulators: it is not healthy to
dream while you are awake, to dream of distant places that are
distant from the daily grind that grinds you down. It is simply an
escape mechanism and escape mechanisms are not healthy; they
are a sign of mental illness in our time. Employers - as stated
previously - also do not like daydreamers; also find them
repugnant to the cause of making money for them, repugnant to
producing for them. You must be wedded to reality, their reality,
the customer's reality, the product's reality, to the economic
reality of realities. But if one does not dream while one is awake,
how can you deal with all the garbage everyone faces in their
daily lives, human garbage thrown at you by humans?

Garbage, dealing with it, how? That is a good question,
answers: drugs, sex, and rock and roll, anything addictive that
makes you think of the addiction and not on life on earth or

humans on earth. I have gone the addiction route, a route chosen during times when I turned from awake dreaming. I have been addicted to indoor gardening, indoor plants, bird raising, Internet bidding on merchandise, collecting things, all things, books, baseball cards, addictions turned to instead of dreaming, beer drinking addictions and they all help until reality hits and boredom hits and then the reality of human life and human garbage and the garbage thrown at you by humans comes through and then reality hits extra hard. Addiction is an impossible device to resort to because it shields you, yes, puts you in a euphoric state, yes, but does so only temporarily and once you realize this, it is too late and the reality becomes more terrible than it would be otherwise and then you run towards the addiction, any addiction again and throw yourself at its mercy and keep throwing yourself at its mercy until it becomes the master and you become the slave until death do you part.

It is better to dream while you awake. You remain the master of your universe. Yes, dream on.

### Thursday, June 28, 2001

Alone in the house in the suburbs again, children at camps, a wife, home for a few days but shopping in the outside world, existing to shop in the outside world and run errands in the outside world. Alone again, naturally.

Thinking about the aging process and something that I have observed: giving up, or, giving up the ghost, or giving up the hope. I have observed it mostly in males, with whom I am a member, but it exists in females, although I have observed it in a lesser degree. Okay, now what do I mean? When you are young, there is hope and with hope new horizons and new people, friends growing, horizons growing with the friends. Great, everything seems like it is in your grasp. At some point, middle-aged point, the world stops growing and begins a solid contraction of hopes, horizons, friends, a shrinking of all as if all has been placed in a hot dryer for longer than specified in the instructions. Sometimes quickly, but usually slowly, the contraction begins, and hopes, one after another, friends, one after another disappear until you are left with yourself before the face of God - if you believe in God. This seems a natural part of aging, but not all accept the aging, some fight the aging, some reach out while aging to remain connected with the world that is in beyond aging, to find new hopes, new friends during aging and sometimes with success. But most, they see, they understand, they accept the contraction, or, at least I accept the idea of contraction, accept that my parents are disappearing, people are disappearing, hopes for my personal future are disappearing; I accept that jobs are disappearing and all hopes of being surprised by anything on earth are disappearing.

Some may say this loss of hope, this contraction of one's world is a matter of personal choice that this contraction is part of a pessimistic world view or part of a personal depression or part of personal cynicism. Possible, maybe, who knows. And that's the other thing that comes with aging, the idea of who knows, only God knows, or somebody else close to God knows. You lose your ability to make definitive judgments about life. So you sit on the fence more while the world contracts more. You sit there and watch as it closes in and realize that this is the beginning of your end on earth, that it is only a matter of time before they are pouring dirt over you or making black ash out of formerly indispensable body parts.

Contraction of life and of hopes, it is all around me, penetrating to my very bone and there is nothing I can do except look at younger people with envy; their world is expanding; their hopes are growing, their friendships forming and blooming with no end in sight. How lucky they are, how lucky. Suddenly I am depressed and need to lie in bed and forget this day; maybe tomorrow my spirits will lift.

## Friday, June 29, 2001

My wife is home with me today, and has promised to spend the time with me, although I now think she wants to back out of the deal. She starts Summer School on Monday so I'll be alone again. I can tell by the way she looks at me that there is pity in her eyes for me, pity by my isolation, lack of friends, lack of a real future; there is also the hidden resentment at being the sole supporter of the family. This all makes sense. Being the object of pity, resented for being pitied, how terrible is the feeling. To have others, family members, outsiders pity you for a lack of future, for your nearing the end, it is debilitating to the mind, helping the process of atrophy further.

This pity is another reason to push other people away from you, as far away as possible, to not share your situation, your fears, your worries, because your fears, your worries, only make them, those outside of you, pity and resent you a little more. And make no mistake about it, pity and resentment go hand and hand, especially in Western societies where. You might think that with pity comes charity, and that might be true, but with pity and the charity comes resentment and the need to remove that source of resentment. You give people Welfare, charity and the next thing you know, society is an uproar about having to give Welfare to the destitute; 'how dare they be out of work, how dare they have children they cannot support, how dare they. Something must be done about them immediately. This situation cannot go on!" Put them, the Welfare recipients, the charity recipients in sub-par housing, give them bags of junk foods produced by the major corporations of the world producing junk, give them unequal access to education and other amenities and then abuse them with words.

Charity, resentment, pity, resentment, self-dignity, non-existent, that is the way and so it is the way to keep the pain inside sometimes, and the pain of unemployment inside as well.

Pity is weakness, weakness is pity and when other humans smell weakness on you, it is like sharks smelling blood in the water. There may be charity given by also attack and destruction and man's inhumanity to man. Take a look at our nursing homes, charity, and compassion, mixed with neglect, disgust, anger even. We feel pity for our elders but also disgust and resentment at their being needy and indigent and without an ability to help themselves. That is the truth. It even works on a global scale. We feel pity for Third World nations, we feel pity for their destitute and starving, we provide charity; but, at the same time, we spit on them, their cultures, look down on their customs, interfere in their rituals and traditional systems, condemn them for their stupidity in not adapting, etc., etc., etc. It is all so very human, pity, charity, condemnation an unending cycle leading to the death of the one on the receiving end and the inhumanity of the one on the giving end.

Well, today I am on the receiving end of pity-charity-resentment and my wife is on the giving end. Out of the goodness of her heart, she plans to spend the day with me, at least until our daughter returns by camp bus at 5:15 p.m. "We can go to the mall and then go to the Indian restaurant and have their buffet lunch; don't you need a few new shirts and a couple pairs of pants." And there are the other errands she needs to make while I am with her, to the supermarket, to the dry cleaner, to hair dresser, to the nail place (for a manicure and a pedicure), etc., etc. I will either wait in the car while she is running her chores or wander the malls going into the look-a-like stores while she is executing her personnel chores. Then, we have to pick up my tuxedo. I forgot to tell you that Sunday, my wife's brother - a lawyer seeking his first fortune before the age of thirty - is getting married up in a fancy upstate area where the girl's family resides. My brother-in-law is currently practicing law at a prestigious Boston law firm; his future wife is practicing engineering at a prestigious engineering firm in Boston; thus, their relationship will be prestigious and hopefully bear much capital that can be used in capital investments of the personal kind.

My brother-in-law's wedding brings up the whole topic of marriage to me, the unemployed adult in the suburbs where I am unemployed. Why did I get married? A bad decision, yes? Most probably so, most probably! I knew then, years ago that I was a bad risk, a writer, unsuccessful into his thirties with no real hopes or leads or any of that other crap, a writer who made his living in the real world as a Technical Writer, writing boring computer manuals for computers he never really liked (notice how I have slipped into the third person here). I also knew then, that I never could keep a job, my life had consisted of jumping from one job to the next, from the next to the next, from the next to the other, from the other to another, on and on we go, a year here, a year there, six months here, six months there. Crazy, a writer hanging on, making no money writing fiction, making a little money writing computer manuals, getting bored in the process, getting fired in the process, on and on and on we go. How could I get married? How could I ever have children? How could I support a wife and family? How could I support myself? Impossible. I knew it then, but disregarded it then; instead, I listened to friends who said it would be all right, to a mother who said it would be all right, to the world which said it would be all right. Well it isn't all right; my fears were founded on flat ground and not on puffy clouds. Since marriage, there have been many job changes, much instability, long periods of unemployment and general destitution. If my wife weren't a teacher with a teacher's union and benefits from that union, we'd all be in the street looking up at the middle classes. If it had been up to me, me, my wife and two kids would be living in the lower echelons of society, be labeled as white trash, receive regular visits from social workers and have to pass stamps for food at the nearest supermarket. We'd be living in some roach infested palace that could catch fire at any moment. I knew it back then, knew I was the worst risk in the world and now I am living proof of it. It makes it all worse, having known and still going through with the wedding, having known and going forth and bringing others down with me. Guilt, shame, upset, I feel all this; how could I do this to my wife, how could I do this to my kids. My kids, there is another topic. What type of example have I been setting for them? Not a good one.

Going out with my wife for lunch today, receiving her charity today. It is all so clear now. God, what have I done?

**JULY 2001**

# WEEK 1

## Monday, July 2, 2001

Alone again. Wife at summer school, kids at camp. House empty. Happy. Sad. An adjustment. Yesterday, was my brother-in-law's wedding. It was at an upstate hotel, very rustic, very sprawling; the place is located along a range of rolling mountains and hills. We went up Saturday and slept over. Nice. My in-laws were there, thousands of people were there, everybody talking at once, congratulating each other at once, everything at once. Hectic, crazy, and I was in the middle of it, me, with my black tuxedo, me, escorting my wife, me, as some sort of central point in all of it, me, myself. Not bad, not good, but look at me today, alone again, in a house, yesterday, thousands of people, bands, wedding marches, people celebrating, today, me, only I, alone with myself, alone with the walls again.

I have always noticed this, the disparity in life, the bloated crowds, the individual sticking out, the solitary individual solitary, the masses pushing and shoving and screaming and talking and hustling, etc., etc., etc. How can any of it be understood? How can you go from suburbia to crowded urbanization in one swell swoop? Driving, I have seen this, driving through overcrowded towns with roads and people and industry, driving through and past and into barren countryside with nothing there, nobody, no thing in sight. The discrepancy is weird. It goes back to the white and black concept, everything in extremes, human beings in extremes and never the extremes meeting in the middle, never the moderation but always the swings right and left, politically, culturally, city and suburbia, swings right and left, extremes everywhere. How crazy is this world. How utterly insane.

I hate the extremes because it makes life difficult, adjusting to the extremes is difficult. Today I must readjust to being alone again and it is even worse than the usual Monday after a weekend of family. Isolation after being immersed in others is horrible; the feeling, it seeps into the bones, saps them of all vitality, eats away at the brain and normal thoughts and leaves you a vegetable, at least for a time; if you are lucky, you recover, if not you wind up looking at yourself in the mirror. I am almost at the mirror stage.

Almost.

## Tuesday, July 3, 2001

Before the national holiday, a holiday of national proportions tomorrow, my wife is off tomorrow from summer school, my daughter is off tomorrow from day camp, I am off because I am off everyday. Holidays no longer have a purpose for me. Holidays, weekends, days merging, one into another, another into one, one into another. This is what it must be like to senior citizens, days coming together without mercy, nothing to break the calendar up, no highlights. Living without highlights, it is a terrible thing, people without highlights is a terrible thing. It is a terrible thing for merchandisers too, those who sell you things, to have people without highlights, the unemployed, handicapped and the senior citizens of the world. Merchandisers love highlights, that is, love the holidays and the festivals when they can sell you things you probably do not need, gifts to fill up the highlighted days, gifts passed from one hand to the next, gifts finding themselves hidden away in basements, gifts eventually brought back to the surface and used as profit-making devices in somebody's garage sale.

Highlights, holidays, religious and national, time-outs punctuating the calendar, days spent beyond work, things that you work for; vacations during these highlighted times, families getting together and reminiscing about previous highlighted time-outs. New merchandise displayed, special foods served, etc., etc., etc. and a day. But being unemployed, it makes no difference to myself; July 4th is like April 12th or any other day in the Christian year. Time is of no essence to me anymore. But it still is a problem because there are the others, those that are still employed by employers who follow time. Thus, tomorrow, July 4th we are going over to my sister's for the traditional barbecue. My sister works, her husband works and thus the highlight time-outs are important to her. She invites other employed individuals to this traditional feast, neighbors and other relatives, all coming to the backyard for burgers and dogs and drink, all talking non-stop because that's what the timeout calls for, a timeout in the middle of their work year.

It means nothing to me, but it means everything to them, the timeouts, the paid holidays from jobs, all of which, reminds me of job interviews and meeting with their Human Resources who invariable - during the course of endless words - get to the particular benefits of the job, including the paid holidays, the 8 to 10 days when the company tells you to stay home and they will continue to give you money for that day. This is important, the timeouts offered here and you make decisions about the job based on the timeouts, that is, you look for jobs with he most paid timeouts that you can find, breaks in the monotony in which you can plan time with the family, vacations around the world, etc., etc., etc. Yes, yes, at job interviews, I sit with the Human Resources individual (usually a female) and listen to them talk about their paid timeouts throughout the year. Of course, the employer is happy to give you these scheduled time-outs and pay you to boot, because they know that you will give that money to other employers - not yours - who sell merchandise that are tied to those time-outs, July 4th, Christmas, New Year's Eve, etc., etc., etc. If I were a conspiratorial type of individual, my God, I could have a field day here, a regular field day. Employers secretly working together, maybe secretly meeting to come up with ways to get the employees of the world to spend and spend and spend and buy and buy and spend in order to support an economy based on buying and spending, spending and buying. But that is all nonsense because employers - money-grubbing fools, no doubt - don't work in unison with anything except their bank accounts and stock portfolios. But, somehow, there is unison, working together of companies that work in economic cooperation to bilk the public of the funds which the companies provide. Make sense, not to me, but the economics never make sense to me. To me it's one endless merry-go-round that never stops even when humans die away.

Timeouts, highlights, vacations, holidays, and the whole business never became more apparent to me then observing my local garden center, often referred to as the nursery. Wow. I am a gardener of plants that love the insides of the home, so watching the nursery, observing it throughout the year has not been hard for me. I go in there, twice, three times a week, wandering about, especially now during times of unemployment. You can set your calendar by the nursery; Thanksgiving and Christmas, decorations to bring in the customers, trees with lights, cider, cookies, hay rides, pony rides, rides and rides some more and tinseled decorations and merchandise everywhere for the season, plants and shrubs and decorations, etc., etc., What about Valentines day and little red hearts everywhere and cupids everywhere and lovey-dovey gifts everywhere and green plants and flowers conveying love (translated money) everywhere. And then there is memorial day and the somber decorations to commemorate the war dead, but memorial day signally also the birth of the gardening season and tomato growing and cucumber growing and annual and perennial growing, a gardening season to commemorate all the money in the bank; and July 4th, a holiday meaning visiting, gifts, garden baskets, barbecue utensils, baskets of geraniums and fuchsias, and all sorts of other things, around the clock, a business conditioned to the paid highlights given out by company's seeking economic vitalization, around the calendar, a business adjusting to the calendar and making money off of it.

Insanity, this is all insanity and I am a part of it. Life, so weird and wild!

## Wednesday, July 4, 2001

Holiday, at sister's house in the suburbs, celebrating with others that live in the suburbs. That's all folks. Enough said.

## Thursday, July 5, 2001

Day after holiday. Alone again, naturally. Yesterday did not go to my sister's house; I pretended illness and managed to get out of it. The thought of sharing my life with my sister and friends, with a cast of thousands, bothered me. I am not in the mood at this point to see anybody, to deal with anybody. I am not in the mood to feign listening to others while they discuss the petty things in life, vacations, restaurants, cars, backyard furniture, their new landscaper, or, worse, their jobs, their important jobs that pay them such terrific salaries that they can afford to go on long vacations to Europe and beyond. Bastards. Let them all go on vacation; they won't enjoy it, they can't enjoy it. What do the middle classes know of enjoyment? They know activities and how to perform them; they understand how to initiate and consummate life's rituals, but enjoyment, that is not the way or the method of attack. They, the middle classes invited over to my sister's backyard are all caught up in the Protestant Work Ethic that even true Protestants don't like anymore. Work will set you free, activity will set you free. Never be idle. Idleness is akin to un-Godliness.

So they make money, so they travel, these people, my sister's friends, people all around me, so they do things, what things. Do they get down and really experience life, or are they doing these things, traveling, existing because they are executing a plan of action that has been planned for them. Pre-packaged lives, pre-packaged jobs and activities, pre-packaged leisure, mass media, vacations, luxury liners, gambling casinos, prepackaged and meant to be executed. We are like computer programs, digitized instructions that are being executed by computers. Life without living, doing without understanding and without meaning. Feeding nothing, giving back nothing. Endless and empty, empty and endless.

Couldn't go to my sister, couldn't leave my house and today I am happier I remained apart. There is also less of an adjustment today at being alone, being separated from others. But the idea of doing, acting, performing activities without feeling, this idea will not leave me. I think this is one of my problems in life, I want to perform activities in life but also want to see the meaning in those activities, i.e., go on vacation and actually see the other human beings with whom I am coming into contact, experience everything about where I am traveling to, learn about where I am traveling to, get my senses to hop up and yell while I am traveling; it is the same with the job, I do not want to only perform it with no thought; I want to experience it, find value in it, let it give me value; I want it to be central to my life. But this is the wrong approach because most jobs do not have inherent meaning, at least in this day and age. People have always told me, just do your job, just do it, do not think about it, do it without thought, just do it. It makes it easier that way. Perform tasks without thought, eat, exercise, work without thought; have sexual intercourse without thought; and, in general,, live eighty to ninety years on earth without thought. Is that what it's all about, going through the motions?

I will not go through the motions. I want to understand everything and feel everything. I will not go through the motions! I refuse even if it means my life!


### Friday, July 6, 2001


Friday, again, Friday, and my mind is blank to match my blank future. It is funny, this mental blankness, or, a blandness. I have no clear insight into myself anymore or my future. I have little idea about anything. Is this depression? What is it? I used to be so clear, so knowing, so confident. No more. I am losing my ability to know what to do about my own unemployment. Used to be, I could redo my resume twelve times in a space of two weeks, send out fifteen thousand resumes and at least get calls from interested parties who wanted to talk but rarely wanted to buy. Now, I can't seem to get my resume together or send out resumes. It has been weeks. What is the problem here?

My focus seems dead. That's right, I cannot seem to focus anymore. It is as if my brain connectors have corroded. I have so many thoughts in my brain, so many ideas of what I should be doing. I have difficulty picking up and running with any of them. There are benefits of being one dimensional in thought, being straight thinking and narrow in scope. My mind is not narrow; it is too broad and I cannot concentrate. I'd like to know why? I have a few ideas. Depression is one answer, maybe I am. Possible. I also think there is that age thing again. As you get older, you accumulate more experiences, more ideas; your thoughts are crammed with lots of information. To choose one idea out of this tangled mass of information, it grows impossible, which makes me laugh about the computer age I find myself in right at this moment in time. You can either call it the computer or information age, and everyone is bombarded with information, if not from the computer, from the television or radio or newspaper or the magazine or from the loudspeakers at the train station, etc., etc., etc. Information is coming at us from every direction; it is a flood that cannot be stopped and there is no place to hide. Now, back to my original idea, that there are too many thoughts, ideas in my head and that has destroyed my ability to focus on any one of them. What of others then? What of the public at large, Mr. Joe Blow and Jane Blow, what of them, and all the information they are bombarded with; do they have trouble focusing in as well, do they have troubling picking out an idea and working with it.

The trouble with a lack of focus is that because you do not have it, you have difficulty getting yourself in motion; sometimes you become paralyzed by inaction. What choice to make, where to go, how to do it, when to do it, ideas, information everywhere, you become a regular information pit unable to process the information, overflowing with information. What information is valuable and what information is not? Questions, inaction, I have ideas, actions I have little of that or little ability to get into action. Am I lazy? Am I confused? How to stop the flood of ideas? How to regain my focus? This I would like to know.

I sit confused.

# WEEK 2

## Monday, July 9, 2001

Monday morning is - as I have previously stated - a depressing time for this unemployed gentleman because I have to get readjusted to being alone during the day; it is also the time of some hope and optimism, a time for a new idea here and there. Now, the new idea here is opening my own business. What a bright shiny idea that is, being your own boss, having the respect of your family and friends as a businessman, on and on. Thinking about it, my chest puffs up with lots of pride and lots of other things that cannot be mentioned here. But what type of business would I open? I have worked in the computer world for years, but I have no ideas there. Could I sell computers? No, don't want to either. Could I fix computers? No, and don't want to. Could I program the computers? No, and of course, I do not want to. What do I want to do with computers? Bury them in the sands of the Sahara and gone on vacation to Bermuda. Joking of course. Sad to say, I have worked with computers - making money here and there - but I still feel ill-equipped to deal with them; translated, I am no expert in their use and care and don't think I will ever be. What other type of business could I open? A bookstore, maybe, but I could never compete with the large book chain stores, never in a million years. Individually owned bookstores are things of the past, relics meant for the dinosaur age. I am a plant expert, houseplants; maybe I could open a houseplant store! Are you joking? How could I ever make a living doing that? Never. Couldn't compete with the chains, or, I would have to combine my garden shop with a florist shop and I don't want to sell cut flowers.

Opening your own business, there are other difficulties, rent, interest, rent, finding the right location, finding the right product, etc. There are all the other factors, facts, things that go against you, a worsening economy, the statistics that say only one out of ten new businesses succeed, over and under, under and over. The world seems to be against you. What can the small guy do? I guess you could always open a liquor store and get robbed, or a candy store and get robbed, or a dry cleaners and get cleaned. But what do I know about running a business like that, or, running any business. I have little knowledge of that or anything else. This makes me laugh because I have all this useless information in my brain but very little practical knowledge or experience. Where has it all gone wrong for me, that's what I would like to know?

Starting your own business, you need the initial capital, which is another word for bread, which is another word for funds, which is another word for money. You need the money not just to start the store, rent the store, buy your merchandise, but you need extra money in the bank to tide you over for the first year or two when you do not make any money. Sick. All seriously sick. So, before I can even start, you are up against all these walls, and chances of success are minimum at best. What is the sense of even trying? Of course, I have seen a few who have succeeded. These are common folk from the middle classes like myself who have hit on a good idea that the public wants and then go with it.

### Tuesday, July 10, 2001

Fighting with wife over money. Where is the money? Where is the money going to come from? Six thousand dollars in expenditure for me in the past few weeks, going to our local suburban school and land taxes, into camp payments, payments for membership in the local Y, membership in the local Temple, membership in the world, pay, keep paying, and today my wife asks for more checks for brick people to redo our steps leading to the house, redo the walkway, redo the driveway, break everything to redo everything, to the tune of $4,000 bucks and she's asking me for it and the reason is clear and simple. She is paying most the other bills right now, mortgage and food bills and entertainment bills, etc., etc., etc. The rest, it is my job, to pay from money I stocked away when working, knowing that I wouldn't be working for that much longer. I have always been that way, put money aside because I always am aware of the lack of permanency of the current job. So there, I have collected some funds and that is what my wife wants me to keep dipping into; and, I also have the unemployment checks from the government, which come to little but are better than nothing at all. But, at the rate I am being tapped for funds, I will have nothing left in my emergency account and I will be the person involved in the emergency.

Money leaving my hands and I am unemployed. What happens to a person when that happens to the person? Money leaving, no money coming in. What happens depends upon the money you started out with. If you are a millionaire, or better, a billionaire, nothing happens to you when money leaves and does not come in, that is, if money doesn't leave you in great gobs. However, if you are poor, or, better yet, middle class, and money leaves and no money comes in, the next step is the end of the American dream, bankruptcy all around, sleeping on the streets all around or, better yet, the charity of the government or some religious institution. Thereafter, you become an indigent, an object of pity to all, and a specimen to be gawked at by school children who are writing reports on the poor.

So money is important because it prevents you from sleeping in the streets in the middle of winter and possibly dying of the elements. If you have money, you will have friends and family; if you do not have money, you will not have friends and family. Those around you will vanish; you will be isolated and without anybody to turn to; without money, you tend to gravitate away from others, others tend to gravitate away from you. The final result, isolation. And it all starts with money, having and holding and caressing and not letting go. And that's why the rich always try to get richer; they fear the reality of not having money, of being without, being thrown out into the cold world, which is really colder than you think, they fear that reality because they understand that reality, somehow the rich understand that better than the middle classes, who never seem to understand anything.

How to deal with the crisis of funds drying up - a nicer way of indicating you are going broke. My inclination is to give up; accept my fate; wait for my wife to give me the boot; for my kids to find another daddy; and, for me, to wander about metropolitan areas of the world alone, in dirty and tattered clothing, asking for handouts from guilt-ridden tourists. Give up, let the world run over you and call it a night. That is the first inclination. But then again, there is something within me that always tells me to fight back, to go out there, to find another job, to try to gather some more paychecks. There is always that, although this is tempered by knowing any such new job is temporary and will soon be lost as they all are.

Money, I must go, I must write a check, a deposit for my son's sleep-a-way camp for next year. A deposit is needed or his space will be lost.

Unemployed and writing checks, my fate, sealed and delivered.


### Wednesday, July 11, 2001


Money, a continuing subject, unemployment checks and beyond, money, a concern but in truth it is merely another human game which is used to pass the time while we are all breathing. Somebody gives you money and you then give that money to somebody else and he or she gives that money to another, so on and so forth. It all amounts to money on paper that is manipulated for pleasure and comfort. Sometimes the money, or money saved, becomes the basis of our feeling secure, which is a laugh because who is secure, who genuinely has their future's lined up and secured, who? You can have the account balance showing big surpluses and all, but in the end, that doesn't stop floods or earthquakes or diseases, or other humans hitting you over the head with metallic instruments. In the end, you are at the mercy of the elements, both human and divine.

I do guess that money does by benefits, figures on paper that show a surplus does buy something; artificial respect, people bowing to you to get a share of those figures on paper, servants waiting on you hand and foot, and stuff that like. It is also reported that you can receive better medical treatment - I believe this but I have seen very rich people die before their time like the rest of us so I tend to disbelieve - and better seats at sporting events, and that you can get into better restaurants, etc., etc., etc. That all makes some sense, but in the end, we are all tragic figures anyway, waiting for the end of time, so does that make a difference. Should be all get nuts because somebody else's figures on paper are better than ours; should we raise the flag of revolution? I don't think so since it doesn't matter very much. We are all just societies of fools who dine on pizza pies and chemical additives; it is the fate of the whole world.

It all comes down to the fact or my feeling of fact that it doesn't matter. This may be my own feeling of lethargy or something of that nature. Lethargy, the way I describe it, is the feeling of who cares. It is not the feeling of 'nothing will work out.' Who cares if this human or that human gets a better slice or the pie or this human or that human gets a better job than myself, who cares if mass media or governments or historical or economic forces are changing around you, who cares about the news of the earth. It is a lethargy of the mind, which may be depression, or, it may be an honest evaluation, meaning, everything you see, people running after figures, people fighting and pushing and shoving, the world of pictures and sounds and all else, don't make much of a difference. The only thing that makes is breathing in and out because when that breathing in and out stops, the world stops, the figures on paper stop, the politics and economics stop, triumphs and tragedies stop.

Lethargy, in this case the mental form, may be the ultimate form of reality programming. You feel lethargy and then watch almost objectively and aimlessly while the world performs about you. There they go, there they do. You nod your head throughout, grin, but do not participate. There is no reality here.

Figures on paper, surpluses, money in the bank, important, true reality, really. Lethargy!


## Thursday, July 12, 2001


Hot out. Barely ever mention the weather, barely. Weather is usually a conversation piece, reserved for a conversation piece between people who meet casually, or, people who have nothing better to say to one another. People at work often talk about weather because that's all they can say to one another that's personal and not business centered. Conversations around the water cooler about the rain or the snow or the heat or the cold, along with frustrated grimaces and various other human gestures.

Hot, being alone, the weather doesn't seem to matter much to me and matters even less being unemployed. Rain or sunshine, the difference is not important. Heat, it is very hot and hot in the house, which makes me feel uncomfortable, which makes me feel more desperate, so the weather is important, but I refuse to discuss the weather with anybody. Which goes to the point that I want to have conversations that are pertinent to daily life, I want to talk with people about how I really feel, how they really feel; I want to discuss my sadness and tragedies and happiness and all the rest and I want them to discuss those subjects with me. I do not want to hear about snow and expected accumulations, or about heat and expected temperature highs. So I guess what I am saying is that I want intimacy, true feelings exhibited in words between human beings. That's what I want and that's what I find lacking. Few people truly communicate. Everything seems to be window dressing, dress the window, see the pretty dressing, forget the items behind the dressing, don't see those items. Isn't that the way it is. We hold these silly conversations about the weather and popular culture, who is going to win the Grammy, Tony, Emmy, who is going to win the World Series, yet, we fail to discuss the truly important things, like why is it that you hate your father or mother, or, have this feeling of inadequacy, or feel the world has past you by, or, do not like your own children, or just are having trouble with the coldness of the world. The weather, the external world, conditions of the external world, concentration on that instead of concentration on the internal world.

Internal world, the world inside the body, the internal world connected with the internal mind of the human, the real workplace of our lives, the real breadwinner in the family. Paradise on earth, where is it, inside, making the internal world come alive, discussing and fixing its problems, paradise arising out of that, human paradise. But it is all avoidance, talking of the weather instead of the personal, not facing the pain and real turmoil, but instead letting it simmer like freshly made tomato sauce.

Casual conversation, conversation about countries, nations, nuclear proliferation, etc., etc., etc., but what of the other conversations of the human soul; what of conversations about humans being alienated from their own bodies, from their own thoughts. The weather, how is it?

## Friday, July 13, 2001

Decided to send out my resume today even though I have heard on the local and national news that the country is heading into recession and there are no jobs and people are being laid-off; of course, this means there will be no jobs for me either; I will be competing against other unemployed human beings and competition does not make me happy; it might make the employer happy, but never me. I rather not compete. I rather just live my life without triumphing over my fellow man. They make you compete, everything is turned that way to make you compete, compete for jobs, compete for a woman, compete to have a family, corporate interests, money interests, other economic interests, make you play this game of competition. Never for a moment are you allowed to breath, never are you allowed to just exist, but instead you are pushed into the game and your neighbors are your competitors.

In this game of competition, you are never allowed to feel comfortable, you are made to look over your shoulder at your competitors who are just waiting for your chance; you are always made to feel insecure, like your job and everything with it may go down the drain. I imagine this is supposed to make you a better worker, more appreciative to your employer, and more appreciative to society in general. What a crock of crap. All their talk, this game they've created for me, all it has done is made me depressed, made me feel like I have no chance, that I will never have a chance, that nobody will ever have a chance. What is the alternative, an alternative that I have chosen? Do not listen to them and their news and their forecasts of gloom, and their ideas centered on competition. Do not listen to their television and radio stations or read their newspapers, magazines or books, do not listen to your fellow man on buses or trains or planes who discuss the ideas that fan the competitive analysis; do not listen to fellow family members discussing it. Listen to nobody except the internal self. Let the world be dead to you.

The resume, I will answer a number of Internet, classified ads, email my resume, but before I do that, I have decided to update my resume, include more current information on it to make myself more attractive to perspective employers. Yes, I have decided to be positive and go out there this Friday and conquer the freaking world. But here I sit and cannot find the words even though I am supposedly a writer. I hate resumes almost as much as interviews. You have to boast upon yourself and all your great accomplishments. You have to say things like: I am a great writer who has produced under tight deadlines, working in the banking and other financial arenas. I have supervised 500 people and personally turned around 500 people and made zillions for my employers, etc., etc., etc. Technically, I am a wizard. I have used and abused xxx software, zzz software, hhh software, etc., etc., ad infinitum plus one ad nauseum." Boasting and lying at the same time. After boasting like this, or, lying like this on my resume or on the actual interview, I somehow feel depressed, deflated, and stupid. It's not that I worry that I have lied about my qualifications and if I get the job, I won't be able to do the job. No, that doesn't concern me because my experience has shown me that most white collar jobs amount to two piles of crap scrapped off the nearest ceiling fan. What depresses me is that my boasting about previous jobs, my lying about previous jobs, makes me remember those previous jobs and how inane those previous jobs actually were. I was there, did little, and learned nothing. It was a waste in every sense of the word. But here I am trying to boast on things that are not worthy of being boasted about. What a situation. I get depressed too because in the larger view, I realize that when I am an old man and look back upon the job situation, I will have nothing to show for it. I will have just been passing time; passing through; period, and end of story.

Of course, realizing the waste is depressing; so I try to imagine that there are millions more, billions more like myself who have wasted it or are in the process of wasting it. Does it make it any better being in a crowd of billions in the same situation as me? Then, again, have I had any choice with the white collar jobs I have had. There is no choice there, just as there was no choice for me in being born into this world where you are made to work at jobs that are lifeless and faceless and for the most part pointless, jobs created for the sole purpose of furthering the economy in some shape or form. I wonder if it had been better if I had been born in farm country and I was a farmer? At least the work I was doing would have a connection to my real life; I would be eating what I produced and others around me would be eating the fruits of my labor. Yes, that might have been better except that in this day and age, huge conglomerate are growing the food; you just pick it or load it into boxes and watch as trucks take the merchandise down the barren highways of the world. What connection is that to the real world? I guess there still is; you can always take pleasure in the thought that the carrots or apples or whatever that you packed are now going into somebody's mouth. Then again, with my luck, I would be working in one of these agro-businesses, one of these conglomerates, but they'd have me sitting in some office somewhere, compiling meaningless statistics on their fruits and vegetables. Alienation would ensure once more, alienation of labor or lack of labor.

I begin re-working the resume. I look at that first job writing computer marketing copy for some software division of some huge accounting firm somewhere and the words fail me. That was a job where I turned out some words I never understood for people I never understood who wore suits and ties and dresses and smelled of cheap perfume. That's all I can remember.

Maybe I can re-write my resume at another time. Maybe on Monday, maybe. Or, maybe I can just leave it as it is. It's good enough. It really is!

# WEEK 3

## Monday, July 16, 2001

Monday morning, weekend spent wandering about the suburbs in my car, while my wife wandered with my daughter - not in day camp on the weekends - in her car shopping. They were running sales at the local greenhouses and I wound up buying a few things here and there, a few pots, a few plants, potting soils and the like; mostly, I just wandered up and down the plant aisles passing the time and wondering about all the people around me, crowds of suburbanites buying for their gardens, spending hundreds each for their annual and perennial gardens, year after year of spending, a spring and summer tradition amongst the suburbanites. I realized too that suburbanites are a breed apart, separated from city dwellers by space and time and mental derivation. City dwellers are looking for pieces of culture; suburbanites are looking for piece of potting soil and ways to use that soil to bury the pieces of culture. A definite gap in wants and desires, I would say.

But there I was, in the greenhouses, roving up and down the aisles mostly aimlessly. As you know by now, I often rove up and back in the aisles of stationary and supermarkets. In fact, if I may, I remember one job, years ago, my first job located in a suburban community where I spent my lunch hours roving up and down the aisles of the nearest supermarket. There was nothing else to do, nothing else to see except green grass, and boring looking, white aluminum-sided box houses. The job itself was located in a gray office park complex, enclosed by a fence that included a series of gray slab buildings, two stories high connected by interconnected roads. The only break was the small reservoir located in the park complex where some ducks hung out. Going crazy there, boring work there, nowhere to go there, I was driven to the supermarket at lunch to view humanity. Who would I see except a few housewives pushing their children along or an occasional female worker rushing towards the deli counter to purchase a salad lunch to take it back to her job at the office complex? But, I would wander sadly in the aisles, stopping to view the different products, reading the label ingredients and wondering if I should make a purchase or not, voting no, and then continuing on again aimlessly, or, making a mental note of the product to then tell my wife about it that night. Aimless, mindless, a passing the time activity, an activity meant to connect me to others, but without success.

Reminded of that job, and now, doing the same this weekend. If my son was back from summer camp, we could at least go to the ballgame together or play stickball together, or do something, drive to the mall and go to the sports store, something, anything and we would talk and I wouldn't be so disconnected. Alone, my wife home, my daughter home, but they going their separate ways, to their stores, their friends, their life, while I sit downstairs, in a room with this computer and with a television set in an adjoining room, alone in the suburbs of my mind. Being alone, dealing with it by wandering aimlessly through greenhouses in my mind, sad but true.

Now it is Monday and I am supposed to get back on the trail of jobs and I am supposed to be redoing my resume, which I cannot muster the strength to do; I cannot muster the strength for anything. I have lined up about ten places to send my resume, found their listings in the Sunday newspapers; they're mostly employment agencies so I do not expect much back. These agencies employ the very young who are transient in nature, never staying at the agency very long, which makes it impossible to develop a relationship with them. Who cares. Life moves on and on and on.

I have this feeling in me again, lethargy, like it doesn't make a difference what I do, that it always turns out the same anyway. Lethargy, it seems inbred in me, a feeling that comes from the thought that all is beyond me, passed my capability that I cannot do, that I can never do. Even as a teenager, others would get part-time jobs after school, I didn't, couldn't. I never thought I could do anything. How could I work a cash register at a store, I was too dump. How could I work in a movie theater taking tickets, too afraid, too afraid of responsibilities, of dealing with others, too afraid that others would make fun of me, too afraid that I wasn't good enough? Thus, my fears caused me to pull back, pulling back caused me to watch, watching caused me to be depressed, depression caused me to be lethargic and dark in approach. It all is so clear and makes such sense. If only I could change it.

Lethargy, the inability to energize, to attack, the inability to attack life the way life should be attacked. No confidence, leading to lack of action, turning into sunken spirits, transforming into sluggishness and mournfulness. It is good to know all this, good to understand, but how can you change this when you have spent your whole life being lethargic.

A Monday with lethargy and no answers.

### Tuesday July 17, 2001

Tuesday, and I did get a call from an agency, particularly from this young headhunter who kept telling me how bad things are getting on the street, how all the jobs have dried up, how he is in danger of losing his job. I listened patiently, though not wanting to listen. I only interrupted him to ask: "Well, I know it is bad out there. But, but do you have anything for me, is that why you are calling?" Silence on the other end, followed by the words, "Yes, of course, I do, a great opportunity."

Amazing, they always tell you what a great opportunity it is, this job or that job, have you noticed that. Opportunity, great, fantastic, going to change your life, make your life a bed of blooming roses or something like that. But when you get down to it, the job is just another job with morons hanging about you asking you, demanding of you, telling you about their deadlines, logging in all your waking hours, monitoring your every movement. This is the great opportunity they talk about, an opportunity laced with tension and acrimony, an opportunity that will take at least ten years off your natural life. If you get enough of these opportunities, you will die tomorrow for sure. I don't believe them when they talk about a great opportunity; I pretend to believe them, however; you have to play the game or else you will be ostracized from the human community, right, play the game, don't speak your mind, nod your head instead of calling them by their true names, by calling attention to the falsity of their claims. We all play the game, we must play the game because human beings like to play games and only like those that will play with them. Those that don't want to play wind up in the jails, mental institutions or isolated and living in some cave somewhere.

Great opportunity. I asked my middle aged headhunter about this opportunity. The great opportunity turned out to be a three week job working in the Pittsburgh area and not even as a writer. The employer - who went unnamed - wants somebody who can use the computer to draw diagrams about their product line and graphs that represent current and past sales of the product. What? Why would he call me? "Well I thought you had used drawing programs on the computer?" "Yes," I answer the dumbbell, "Yes, I have but only in the course of my work as a writer. I am a writer." He grunted at me, apologized to me, asked me again if maybe I could do it or if I knew anybody else that could do it and then quickly left the phone line and went off into the oblivion of time and space.

Being called by these morons, job search people, headhunters, it is a fascinating thing. They call, get friendly with you for a minute or two, want to know all about your life and then disappear two minutes later into oblivion never to be heard from again. I always assume there has to be some philosophical ideal behind this or something. To have all the attention on you and then no attention on you, to be a public figure and then an anonymous clown. That's how great Hollywood stars who are no longer Hollywood stars must feel. First they cannot get away from their adoring public and the next moment, their adoring public is nowhere in sight. How upsetting is that. How weird is that. It is better to be anonymous for all time rather than be famous for part of the time and anonymous the rest. Feeling of being abandoned, ignored, rejected, they are all bound to follow this adoration-ignore process. And that's how these headhunters make me feel, adored and then ignored. They call, praise me for my background, promise to help me towards a better future, say I deserve a better future, and then nothing. I call them back a day later, a few hours later and they no longer know who I am or even recall my name. Is that bizarre, or am I bizarre.

Human beings, I hate them sometimes.

### Wednesday, July 18, 2001

I have decided to be upbeat, at least for the day. I have decided to re-think my thinking and look at the world from a rosier perspective. All these dark thoughts, all this acrimony directed at my fellow man, what does it accomplish except to make it bitter. What is the phrase, what you put in is what you get out, garbage in/garbage out. Yes, I must think happy thoughts towards my life and those around me and my life will suddenly look and feel better. Let's try it.

Rather than see my upbringing, my father - often unemployed and other times mean or drunk - as a great man, a misunderstood soul who really had great vision that was never truly recognized. Here was a man of culture and religion who sought only the best for his wife and children, who loved his brother and sisters to a fault, who personally isolated himself in order to raise himself to the level of helper of mankind. And here I am his son.

My mother, not the bossy, opinionated woman that you have been led to believe, not involved in making others decisions for them, but a person seeking only the rectification of the human condition from humans, a female savior seeking to save the population from the need to make individual decisions. What a mother to me and my sister, always there, always kind, always supportive, encouraging education and all other true endeavors in life. And family and friends, wonderful individuals, there whenever I need or needed them, never abandoning me in times of need, like during this time of unemployment. And my wife, never concerned only with herself and her needs and her goals and getting and staying ahead as a teaching professional seeking to be a principal and member of higher boards of education, no, an individual caring and passionate for others, me, her children and their futures. Yes, yes, yes. Shall I go on?

Cannot go on because it isn't true. I cannot help seeing the darkness because the darkness is everywhere around me; darkness infects my soul, every day a little more darkness, every day turning the remaining bright spots in my soul, dark and dirty. When you get down to it, there isn't anybody you can ever trust, not even your own parents. Everybody is out for themselves, trying to push you down into the quicksand of life. Dog eat dog, that is the operative world. Garbage in/garbage out, maybe we are all born to garbage that is perfumed by thoughts to appear as something else. Maybe what we perceive as beauty, art, religion, morality, is really only window dressing and the reality is something entirely different and dark. Maybe that's why there are human beings who commit suicide, human beings who have diseases and wish only to die, human beings who are old but cherish the age as a step closer to death; maybe these people understand the basics of the darkness, maybe they can see and feel it like I can see and feel it.

Your fellow man, what if the smiles and the kind words are simply false statements of another reality. Maybe those science fiction movies where the people turn into monsters or zombies or ugly looking serpents are not fiction but the true reality. What if our manners, our ways of life are only masks of the horror that lurks beneath. Just because the horror is papered over doesn't make the horror go way. Though somebody might smile at you, they can still kill you with a knife or gun or with your bare hands. Living your life to be cautious, that is the only way, living your life always on the ready to defend yourself that is the only way. Why are people like this? Why so vicious? People are not vicious consciously, but down deep, we are all still animals, hunters, grasping for position, willing to push our fellows out of the way for our own chance. Animals, humans are animals and no matter what the church says or what the minister says, we are still the same, low-down dogs who walk on two legs. But saying that, there is hope. If only we were honest and admit to the fact of our low-life natures, we would cease to be hypocrites and would act and perform as all animals do, logically, like dogs or lions or whales, existing in nature as we should. It is the pretension that causes problems. It is when we expect people to behave like Gods that we get into trouble, it is when we expect others to act by some moral code that we get into trouble, get disappointed, make judgments, seek retribution, and thereafter, act in an inhumane manner.

Men are base dogs. I admit that. I totally do and with that admission, I set myself free.

### Thursday, July 19, 2001

I pick up my son from sleep-away camp next week, or, shall I say that my wife and I pick him up next week from summer camp, drive for hours through the city and into the woods and there drive up mountains and then find him through a thousand campers and counselors, load all dirtied belongings and there we have it. Driving through a city to the country, driving onwards and upwards and observing the landscape changing. Why does this remind me of the time I was with my wife many years ago in Egypt, and driving through Cairo in a bus into the countryside, in a bus, and remembering seeing marshes and remember being told to watch the Cyperus trees from which the first paper was made, the water, the plants in the water, the smell, weirdness, everywhere. The city, so filled with humans, the countryside so devoid. Again this brings up the disparity in life, sterile on one side and fertile on the other side; good on one side, bad on the other; black to the core, white to the essence, health, sickness, birth, death, beauty and degradation, city, country, wild, tame, disparity everywhere which goes beyond the human disparity. Why can't everything be balanced in life? Why can't there be some middle ground? Why do there have to be extremes?

I just want to live my life on an even keel without the ups or downs, the high and lows, the emotions hitting heights and depths. Why can't I do this? Is that my problem? Is my problem that I am looking for a situation that doesn't call for extremes, where a job doesn't call for extremes? As I get older, I have trouble dealing with others who are too sad or too happy; I have difficulty in dealing with the angry and the uplifted. I look at others who are in a state of delirium at hearing good news, and walk away as quickly as possible. Extremes. Moods, swings of emotion, and I fear always getting caught in the backlash. Not reacting, that is what I attempt to do. Sitting there, trying not to form opinions, not to form emotions, remaining neutral even in terrible successes and failures, this is what I try to do. I refuse to be a yo-yo of emotions and extremes. I refuse to be sad at tragedies, do not wish to fall to the depths, because from the depths I will invariably rise, and go in the opposite direction. In the end what you get is a cycle of emotion, a cycle of black and white, endless, driving, sick, destroying everything that is normal and good in life; translated, the state to shoot for is tranquility where very little happens at the extremes, where most things take place in the middle.

How did I learn my lessons? The hard way, folks, the hard way. My father was a man of extremes. One day happy, delirious in delirium, uplifted, the next minute, angry, violent, immoral, and brutal to others around him. Never did the two meet; the two extremes never shook hands. Living, you had to learn to recognize the extremes and then try to deal with each. I learned to deal by not reacting to the extremes, resisting his joy and morality and his anger and immorality; both were equally false, both negative. That was the hardest lesson of all to learn, to not get drawn into his contagious happiness. I learned that once I got sucked in there, I would get sucked into the lows, the anger, the despair and then my life would just be one roller-coaster ride away from insanity. The goal, as taught to me by my dear old father, is to try to be as constant as I can be, to be as level as I can be. Do you know why? Well, it is simple, and put simple, goes something like this: to be level, to avoid the extremes, means you can deal with life without extremes, you can deal with your fellow human beings without the extremes and all life on earth without extremes; you can avoid overly praising, overly abusing those around you, even the family dog; you can avoid the violence and the meanness, the flattery, the false smiles, the inhumanity, etc., etc. The goal should be to deal with the world around you in a sane way. To do that you must avoid going between the North and South Pole in your mind constantly. But, often you will be told this is not possible, often you will be told that you must choose between the North and South Pole, between the darkness and the light; religion often tells and teaches this very thing. It teaches you to be unbalanced, at least the Western religions do, it teaches you to battle one, to defeat one, the darkness, in order to come to the light. The basic essence of this is that you can always live in the light, in the good; you can always live in the extreme. This is a lie of course, the good and the bad, they go together. Unless you can eliminate the bad forever, you will forever be balancing between your good and your bad. There is no such thing as being with God all the time. The Devil will have its due. Religious people, monotheists will say something different. I say, the best state to be in is one where you are between the darkness and the light, God and the Devil, where you can see both sides, understands both sides without making judgments about either. It is a balancing act but one worth taking for the soul. No choice but to live in the middle. I must. I have to. Otherwise, I cannot live and wouldn't want to.

### Friday, July 20, 2001

Politicians, my mind is turning toward national politics. Is this peculiar or not. Do you see me as a political creature? Not really. But I turned on the TV to one of those news channels and there were these white male politicians, you know the type, a little overweight, slicked back hair, wearing suits and ties and smiling pompously into the camera while speaking pompously into the camera. They were being asked questions about the national economy, the weakening stock market, the current rising unemployment rate, etc., etc., etc., and they kept smiling as they answered that the country, was not in a recession or God-forbid a depression, not now; it is simply a brief economic downturn while the economy turns around. Promised they, in a few months, everything will be better, people will be better, jobs will be better and more plentiful. This time is a brief respite from the sizzling economy. The economy just needs a little time to cool down before turning hot again.

Promises, politicians, inherent story-tellers who will tell stories for people who in return hold them either in high regard, ill regard, but who hold them, listen to them as their spokesperson while at the same time knowing that these politicians are self-serving, politicians self-serving throughout history, kings, and queens, and parliamentarians, judges, senators, etc., etc., etc., and more etc. Politicians all the same, all seeking to place themselves on a platform, all seeking to turn certain truths to their advantage, all seeking to get the advantage for themselves, advantages gained sometimes with ruthless consequences, sometimes with more benign consequences, but always with consequences. They speak, I listen, but I filter my hearing to try to really understand. Economic slowdown, meaning what? What are they saying, really? Why won't they come out and say recession/depression? It doesn't serve their interests. It sounds too bad. But what of the thousands losing their job and the thousands who are about to? What would they call it, a minor economic slowdown or something worse? We know the answer. If only the politicians would admit the truth, if only. I would feel better also; people would stop asking how I could be unemployed in the twenty-first century. I could just point to the reality. But you know the one thing about reality, if people don't talk about the reality, the reality doesn't exist, at least not in their head. Reality is what we make it and right now recession/depression is not what we make it. But why go on about this, specifically, why go on about politicians, these individuals who like to preside over us and beat their own drum. They are here to stay along with cancer and heart disease. They have always been here and will always be here just as humans continue to walk the heavenly earth.

Yes, politicians will always be with us and recessions/depressions will always be with us and have always been with us. There always have been good times for the economy and bad times for the economy. Translated this means that there have been good times when humans had adequate food and shelter in abundance and there have been times when that hasn't been the case. For farmers depressions are when their crops fail or the price of crops fall and they cannot make a living and they cannot pay debts and farms are sold by bank executives who will soon be out of work themselves. For businesses, it is a time when their products don't sell or don't sell adequately, it is a time when luxury goods don't sell, intellectual property is ignored, etc., etc., but you get the message, lots of people in need, although never all the people. A few prosper, always a few for reasons never really clear. Often times the people who do prosper are not particularly bright or attractive or worthy in any philosophical sense. Maybe they are just ruthless, willing to do anything to keep their wealth, though, this is particularly true either; I've seen the rich in bad times, depressing times, and some are not ruthless at all, some are just non-entities like the rest of us. Inherited money, not as much in this day and time, where inheritance goes thousands of ways into the wind. Who know; who cares.

I have lived through these economic downturns and economic upturns; I have worked through them, been unemployed through them and always marveled at them. Why marveled? How people react to them makes me marvel. People see the good times and the bad times equally. In either case, they see no end in sight. They are hopeless during hopeless times and jubilant during times of jubilation. There is that certain lack of vision that comes from only seeing what is in front of your nose. What results are either people who are depressed and live like dogs that have been beaten with a stick or like optimistic fat cats who live to show their wealth and prosperity. The highs and the lows are always there and people's behavior is always there. My view, it is best to ignore the economic highs and lows, just go about living, as simply as possible being neither pessimistic nor optimistic.

Salvation, mine, depends upon the middle position, maintaining                                                                                     it.

WEEK 4

**Monday, July 23, 2001**

Tomorrow my son returns from sleep-away camp. He will be home for a few days thereafter and start at a day camp thereafter for a number of weeks; the camp allows him to choose a specialty and he has chosen baseball. Okay. Got it. My daughter is continuing at day camp, got that. She comes home from camp every day on the bus, eats dinner and goes to bed. She says she hates the camp, has no friends at the camp; that's all she says. My son has always said he hates camp, any of the camps we have sent him to, and has no friends at these camps. Year after year, we send the kids to camp, we spend at least $10,000 a summer on the camps, and year after year, they hate them. Why do we do that? We do we spend such a sizeable part of our income on entertaining our kids for two months? Ask my wife. She's the one who says that it is essential for their development, she's the one who makes the decisions to spend big chunks of the money, money I can longer earn being unemployed and without prospects.

Why send them to camp? Why spend such a fortune that cannot be afforded when I am often unemployed as I am at the present moment? Why? Her reason: 'You must keep the children active, doing, never bored; boredom is the devil's child. It is the same reason she enrolls the children in dance class, baseball and bowling leagues, girl scouts, wrestling leagues, chess leagues, keep them active and out of trouble, especially here in suburbia where trouble is just around the corner. Does this work with human beings in general, keep them busy, keep them doing so they cannot think because when humans think that's when there is trouble, that's when they get off the beaten track, that's when they question the values around them, that's when they can point to the vulgar materialism of their society. God forbid that happens. You cannot let that happen. Society cannot let that happen. If that happens you will have a nation of teenage revolutionaries roaming the streets. God help us all. They will bring down our cherished institutions of government and religion; they will bring down our malls, places where an endless string of products are thrown at the public at large. Cannot let kids think, not for the moment because thinking might make them question, and questions are better left to greater minds.

Letting others think for us and question for us. We let the intellectuals do our thinking and questioning, we let our media people - reporters, announcers, moderators, etc., etc., etc. - do our questioning. The trouble is most of the people we allow to question have sold out their values years ago and bought into the pre-existing system. They are part of the problem and not the solution - where have you heard that before. The bastards in charge and doing our thinking are paid to think in certain ways and to uphold certain values. There is no doubt about it. They are paid to sift through the real reality and come up with the reality that is not the real reality. They are paid to uphold the government, the religion, the corporate culture, paid. The moment they diverge from the party line, they are excluded - it's a one in a million shot for them to diverge. Now, when they diverge, police don't come to the door to take them away, soldiers don't come to exile them to a Siberia, the government doesn't put them in their Federal prisons, none of that, not in a free society. What happens when they diverge, they simply are excluded. Editors no longer take their work, producers no longer hire them; they are left out of the process, the reasons given being popularity. As they are no longer popular figures, they are not marketable, meaning they no longer produce profits, profits which fuel the system and the popular taste.

Thinking when done outside the scope of the popular is never condoned, can never be condoned. Thinking can be condoned only by the elite few who are condoned, who are endorsed by the system. Others are expected to have these few think for them. For these others, the children, the adults, there is the opium of the masses, religion, music, sports, activities, never ending activities, work activities that usually mean nothing, sports activities, clubs, bars, noise everywhere, everywhere and never ending.

Inactivity is the devil's child. Keep busy everybody, keep busy!

### Tuesday, July 24, 2001

Son camp home from camp, in a bus, a yellow bus; bus dropped son off at a suburban school thirty minutes from our home. Son had his belongings, bags, son smiling, happy, asked to go to hamburger joint when he saw us, asked for pizza when he saw us, us to go to a fast food Mexican joint when he saw us, asked for presents when he saw us, me and his mom. Home, my son is now home for a few days with me before he starts day camp next Monday. While he was away, got him a new computer system for his room; I didn't tell you that, but we got it for him from my unemployment checks, set it up in his room, with my unemployment checks, bought games for his new computer, from my unemployment checks, and he now is playing with his new computer, playing the games, going to the Internet, his door is closed and he is playing and going to the Internet; his television is on, switched to a baseball game while he plays his games and goes to the Internet.

I was looking forward to my son being home to keep me company, but am disappointed because he seems to just want things and not people, not me. He wants his food and comforts, and not me. Who needs me? Not my wife and daughter who are completely independent of me. My son was one of my last hopes, but he just needs the things. Maybe I have an importance in that I provide the things that he wants. But what happens when he is able to provide those things for himself; I will become an afterthought, a non-essential. Maybe that is the way of it. You must be realistic in life, especially about those immediately around you. You must be able to look through the gratitude and the warmth and see the other things, like the ingratitude, being ignored by them, being forgotten by them, the selfishness, etc., etc., etc. I see my son now, eleven years old and dependent upon myself, but visualize him at twenty or thirty, or forty, living in another part of the country, calling me once and a while on my birthday for a brief moment or two and then forgetting me just as soon as he's off the phone. He will have his own wife or wives and children and be doing his own thing with his own hobbies. Who cares about a father, that thing from the past who used to buy him things, who cares one bit. Does it sound like sour grapes, maybe it should, and maybe it shouldn't. It's the American way, however, and slowly becoming the international and cosmic way. The disintegrating family unit, an old story now, each and every one of us living longer so that we can die alone in some old age facility eating apple sauce and being cared for by fat old nurses aids who care not for you but only about when they get off for the day. That is the way.

Maybe that the knowledge that I will be abandoned by my son is good knowledge. I long ago understood that I was already abandoned by my wife and daughter. Whether I lived or died, their lives would go on without a blink. My daughter eight is reliant now on her mother and in a few years will be reliant on nobody. She laughs at me a lot, kisses me, draws pictures for me, but in the end is distant from me, related to me only through some genetic accident of fate. My son, also in the world, though he is not aware of it either. If I weren't here, he'd do well, just as well, with his computer and games and Internet connections, etc., etc., etc. Depressing thoughts but real ones. Some of us know the basic truth of the matter, and the truth is that we are not essential. If the world can continue without Einstein and Jonas Salk and Aristotle and Julius Caesar, and all the others that have made some sort of contribution, it certainly can go on without us. The world will not even skip a beat, not even miss a beat. Time and activities does not stop for anybody.

While participating in the world it is always good to keep this in mind, the world revolves with or without you. With this in mind, you will never make a fool of yourself, or let your ego run rampant, or let your greed run rampant, or, your religion run rampant. Yet the knowledge will not make your life easier; in fact, your life becomes more difficult, more depressing. It is easier to live thinking you are the center of the universe and that the universe is dependent upon your continued survival. As a consequence, you will be richer in the world, more filled with material possessions, smile more, have more power over those around you, being a civic leader, etc., etc., etc. But in the end, it is a lie. Nobody is the center, no human beings. We are just bags of bones that when sold at auction will garner three or four dollars in return. We are basically worthless, to be forgotten over time even when our headstones are deeply engraves with dates of birth and date and a little saying here and there; headstones disappear too overtime like mountains and valleys disappear over time.

Religious people would say that God does not disappear over time, that God is eternal and represents eternal salvation. That is where the permanence lies; God doesn't fade; God isn't ephemeral like human beings. Put your faith in God or if not God, in some religion or ideology and you will not pass, you will leave your mark on the world and attain some sort of permanent condition here that will make life meaningful. Okay, that does sound good, splendid in fact, just splendid, but it takes a leap of faith to believe any of this. It takes putting aside the rational side and that is a big jump that few of us really can make. I cannot. I cannot move beyond the proofs of my own observation and the rules of science. Perhaps that is my own failing.

Permanence, some people see permanence in genetic perpetuity, that is, in having children and their having children and their children having children in one great chain leading back to you. The problem is that after one or two generations of this chain, you are forgotten, dead to your descendents for the most part, and no longer a spec of dust in anybody's cerebellum. That is the way.

In the end, you just have to prepare for the end of it, the end of time, your time and be prepared and armed with the knowledge that you are in the end a worthless dolt who exists briefly and then nevermore.

## Wednesday, July 25, 2001

My son, today, it is him and me, my wife at work, in summer school, my daughter still in summer school. My son complaining, he is bored, nothing to do around the house, around the neighborhood, no friends for him, no nothing for him. What do I expect, that he sit in front of his new computer and play computer games all day? Is that what I expect him to do? That's really boring. My son doesn't want to be bored, cannot be bored and looks to me as the entertainment committee of one, which is a great joke since I've been bored for years in this suburbia backwater. He wants me to entertain him. I make suggestions. Let's go to the mall? Boring. Let's go to the hardware store? Boring. Let's take a drive? Boring. Let's go into the city and bum around? Boring. Everything to him is boring. I laugh. He starts his day camp next Monday and then won't be bored while I still have a lifetime of it left.

In that I envy my son, that is, I envy him that his life is not one long stretch of boredom. There will be the new schools, the new friends, the new woman, and the new careers, to break that boredom up. Eventually, however, the ultimate reality will set in, the reality being the ultimate sterility of it all. My son will face what we all face, walls all around, lacking meaning, lacking adventure, my son will face the regular routines of life that naturally kill imagination and make living into a black hole.

Joke. He looks to me to turn the boredom off and the adventure on. He is young yet and will have to learn that I do not know how to do that. If I could end the boredom, I would. If I could make everyday life interesting, I would. People make life interesting by creating situations; at least I think so, create emergencies and catastrophes, murder one another and rob one another to break out of the boredom box, to make things a little different for them. But even then, ultimately we return to the box. Prisoners return to their prisons and homeowners return to their sterile homes with their walls and piped in music and television images. Plain lives, lives of routine, lives planned without much hope.

How can a person really make life less boring? Is life boring for everybody? I don't think so. There are people who say they are never bored, that life is the ultimate adventure. Are these people lying? My wife is rarely bored, come to think about it. There are all her friends, acquaintances, teacher friends, family of teacher friends, constantly calling the house, she is constantly talking on the phone to them, constantly talking about other people; my wife is constantly going to the supermarket or to the cleaners or to meet this one or that one for lunch, constantly meeting with this parent or that parent, constantly planning a next activity, take the my so to this doctor or that doctor, take my daughter to this doctor or that doctor, then to dance practice, then to guitar practice, take them, bring them back, talk to parents, schedule them for activities, schedule herself for activities, and throughout she is never bored, never in need or search of activity, never within that boredom box.

My wife, not bored, certain people never bored, I envy them since I am always bored, bored when I am employed and bored when I am not employed. I see no way out of this dilemma. So maybe I am jealous of my wife and the others like her who seemingly find meaning. But have they found meaning in all of this or is it all illusion that I am buying into to, a sham of sorts. The basic key I think to their lack of existing within the boredom box is they never think of the box, never think of the boredom, and never admit that boredom exists. They focus on individual actions, physical activities that need be performed throughout the day. They do not wonder, think, ponder, nor do they pontificate, question, ask, delve, they do, perform, generate. There is no boredom because there is no time for it. Life, performance, that is the ultimate goal. And these people, my wife included, are very much like animals; animals never get bored because they are too busy just trying to survive, looking for food, looking for shelter, etc., etc., etc., except if they are common pets, dogs and cats and birds and alike who can get bored just sitting there and need toys and added stimulation and such. So we should qualify ourselves, when discussing animals because we are strictly speaking of wild animals. Wild people then, those who perform, do, move about without thought of boredom, they are wild also.

If I was an employer now, thinking again of employment, I would always hire the wild ones, those that never exist within the box or even think of the boredom box. My first question on the interview would be: Do you ever get bored? If the answer is no, I know I have a winner there, a productive adult who will keep producing until they drop without questioning what they are doing. Questioning is sometimes indicative of boredom; you question because you are bored; you are bored because you are thinking while performing an activity. Performing most functions today, most jobs, one must not think, at least not in a philosophical sense, one must just do, do, do, perform, act, perform some more and then go to bed and get up the next day and do the same. This goes for everyone from the brain surgeon to the carpet cleaner. Performance without thought, activity without questioning, that is the key.

So there, I have it. But how to deal with my son's boredom of today. I have it. There's a Yankee baseball game this afternoon at the Stadium, an activity. I put the activity in the form of a question. Yes, he wants to go. The boredom is gone. The activity triumphs.

For now, the activity does triumph, for now! But what about tomorrow?

### Thursday, July 26, 2001

Boredom, again my son and dealing with it. We went to Yankee Stadium yesterday to deal with his boredom; I bought a computer for him to deal with his boredom and games to go along with it to deal with his boredom. And now I have reached a conclusion about boredom, it costs a lot of money to deal with it, or to keep it away from your door.

Think about it, boredom is expensive to deal with. In fact, it has created cottage industries that have grown into major industries. Spectator sports, electronics, computers, television, radio, telephones, industries of communication and industries of boredom. The mass media, electronic games, going to baseball games and rooting for your favorite stars, all measures to meet boredom and the boredom of life, all measures to meet and deal with it, to tackle it, all activities created to be executed to deal with it.

Mass media, time passing, time killing, movies, time killing, time passing, sports, the same, electronics, the same. Sometimes these things, they make life simpler, an electronic can opener for example, but sometimes they are there just for the entertainment value, and the entertainment values is there to break the boredom. The problem is the expense, because, again, breaking the boredom, finding activities, instruments to break the boredom, is expensive, which is where capital comes in and the capitalists, who cater to the need at a goodly price.

Is it the fear of boredom that is a driving force? There are those who never get bored - we said that already. But there are those who do, and others who don't but fear being. Thus, the great cottage industries are born out of fear of boredom, and the great inventions are born out of it, and the great pastimes are born out of it. The great war we as humans face is not against hunger, it is not against sickness, it is against boredom and ridding it from our shores. Get rid of boring tasks, let machines and computers do those, get rid of the repetitious, let technology handle that, free up the human for more interesting tasks, free up the human mind to more interesting developments, etc., etc., etc.

I think or I guess that this is all fine, sure, great. But boredom costs as I have previously stated and my son's boredom costs plenty. Every time he is bored, dollars go flying in every direction for tickets, admission charges, electronics, money flying off in the direction of the modern economy to the point where you cannot earn money quickly enough to make up for the losses.

This all leads me to say: what's wrong with being bored in life; I know when I am bored, I turn into myself, and once I do that, I begin to think, to try to understand the world, myself, others around me. Once I am bored, I get my focus back and focus on the important things in life, those around me and my relation to that. There can be pain there in the recollections that follow and in the honest evaluations of self that follow, but so what. Pain leads to growth, which leads to a better individual, which leads to humanity advancing morally.

But maybe I am wrong. Maybe we should never get that chance to think or feel. Maybe we should never be bored, have time for boredom. Maybe. Somebody else may have the answers. Maybe.

### Friday, July 27, 2001

Friday rolling around again, no job, no prospects and next week, it is already August. Interesting. Summer is half over and there is nothing for me that I can see. August coming. Wasn't the name August named after his imperial majesty Augustus Caesar? Think so just like July which was named after his imperial majesty, Julius Caesar. Interesting facts, I can always give you facts read from books. I am good at trivial facts, excellent in fact with the facts. I am well read in history and literature and can relate things that few people can, dates, times, places, going back to five thousand years ago. But when it comes to practical knowledge that brings in practical money, I am not such a scholar. In fact, I am a downright fool, idiot, moron, and jerk off the street. The dog catcher or the fireman, garbage collector is of more use than I. This is a statement of truth and self-evaluation, which I have some talent about.

Growing up it was book reading that was my natural sport rather than other sports like baseball, football, running after women and the like. I liked the inside of my own room, reading my own books, learning history, memorizing history, pondering the historical process that was me. While the neighborhood kids existed in the outside world, I existed in the inside world of the interior lobes of the brain. Was this good? Was this bad? A value judgment, please! Good or bad. It would have been good if I had ever chosen to use the knowledge learned in books in some practical manner, but I never chose to do so. I could have gone on in academia beyond graduate school, but just couldn't get along with people enough, with institutions enough to do so and become a college professor and beyond. The same goes for becoming a teacher. I could never get along with others enough, nor had enough confidence to find permanent employment as a teacher, although I have dabbled in that field over the God-forsaken years.

Practical knowledge, I lack that, book learning, I do not lack that, knowledge of facts of human history, I do not lack that. What is all my reading, my study of history and literature come to? What is it worth? I can relate facts about the Crusades, the Spanish Inquisition, Napoleon's landing in Egypt, but I cannot get a job. I can discuss the works of Charles Dickens and Mark Twain, yet I can't get a job. I cannot use my learning. I am stunted, stifled, and unsure how to deal with the world as that world exists more in a practical and not theoretical sense. Using something, you must use what you learn in books and school, isn't that correct? What you do not lose, you lose? Is that not correct. How is it that I have this whole base of knowledge and nowhere to go with it? I remember at previous jobs, sitting there behind a terminal hitting keys on a keyboard that have nothing to do with my real base of knowledge and then wondering why. Others have wondered why, why a guy with some much trivial knowledge is sitting in the middle of a sterile office, pounding the keys on a keyboard and not using the trivial knowledge.

I guess the operative word then is trivial. Trivial means secondary, of less importance and whether I can talk about 'The Pickwick Papers' or not is of secondary importance, whether I know when and how the Normans conquered England is secondary. But what is trivial. Something that is not useful, I guess would be considered trivial. But there is more to it than that. Trivial, at least defined in this society, is something that does not have economic ramifications; in other words, it is something that doesn't carry economic importance, in other words, something that doesn't make a buck. Something isn't trivia or trivia when you can make a buck with it. Knowledge for knowledge sake is trivial.

So I have to think of my knowledge within the great economics of economics and come to the conclusion that within, the knowledge is trivial, but from outside the economics it may not be trivial. There is a thought in my head, however, which is related, about trivia and the reason why I live; do I live to help and support other individuals? Maybe. What is my knowledge, the knowledge learned from books, how has that helped others? It has not. My knowledge, all the facts and details, have helped nobody and thus have not even helped myself. Thus my facts are trivial and trivia. Depressing thoughts.

All the time spent growing up, reading, studying were for nothing. Those who participated in the world, who never picked up a book but were doing, they were the smarter for it; I was the stupider for it. Those years of study, learning trivia, were wasted years, years burned in the wasteland of thought. I could have been out there, making friends, participating in sports, acting as a typical teenager, delighting in the opposite sex, delighting in the good things that the world has to offer, but instead, there I was behind closed doors concentrating on human fact that add to nothing, that can help nothing.

But maybe, thinking some more, there is no such thing as trivia and trivial, maybe there is not merit in participating with other, no merit in being a teenager and gaining practical knowledge of the world. Maybe practical knowledge isn't worth it, maybe humans aren't worth it. Maybe being alone in quiet contemplation was not so bad. Maybe my youth of reading and learning wasn't misspent. Maybe.

Unemployed, wondering, about my, youth. Thank God, the weekend is coming again.

# WEEK 5

## Monday, July 30, 2001

Son, out the door, a day camp beginning for him. Adjusting to being alone in the house, daughter still in camp, wife teaching at summer camp, adjusting to loneliness and alienation, adjusting to the sound of my own voice and the sound of my face, being alone, trying to deal with it, getting through it.

Have the classified ads in my hand from the New York Times, but they are very thin, thin pickings. It's been like this all summer, nothing in the paper for me, nobody wanting me, nobody calling me except a headhunter or two and they call only to discover if I am still breathing. This brings up another interesting point, the time I am out of work becomes a black mark, one that will be questioned in the future when I do have an interview and people question you at that moment in time. "So you have been out of work three months? Why? Was this of your own choosing?" Questions like this, suspicious, people wanting to know, to understand why nobody will hire you. Is there something wrong with him? Is he a problem at work? Is he incompetent?

Stupid, fools, jerks, incompetents. Why don't they understand that getting a job when there are no jobs available is an impossible task? Impossible. Recession, depression, no calls, no desires, and you are alone. Why don't they understand that I have not caused my own calamity, that I sit here in suburbia without work or friends or acquaintances, amidst streets desolate by day, and it is not of my own doing? I have not caused my own downfall, disintegration, decay. Why do they blame the victim and not the victimizers? I don't understand. And as the months of unemployment goes on, and the time goes on, their questions just grow meaner and sterner. I will have to deal with this by lying; pretending that the time between jobs has been minor, that is, lying about unemployment, fiddling with the dates of the matter. What is the alternative, listening to their words and their accusative eyes?

So here I sit on the couch with the classified ads from Sunday in my hands and a black pen in my hands and here I am ready to analyze the ads and circle the ads and then go to the computer with my ads and send out my resume electronically to those ads, here I am, myself, me. I have been sitting with want ads for twenty-five years now, even when I have had jobs, I have been sitting with want ads, usually on Sundays, but now on Mondays, sitting and circling and deciding and circling, and wondering and circling and then posting and addressing and sending and then waiting and then eventually hearing and talking to strangers on phone who are asking personal questions, monetary questions and usually passing into the night. And here I am again, this is my life again and again and again, and it is boring and depressing, leaving me with the feeling of never progressing, never having progressed. I am sick and tired. I hate Mondays; hate them since they bring the same thing to my life, that certain sense of utter hopeless.

I am going to take a nap now, will put down my want ads and hope to sleep it all away as one can a bad dream.

I pray I can.

### Tuesday, July 31, 2001

Is that sense of hopelessness permissible? Am I permitted to feel hopeless, or, is this part of mental illness. Am I mentally disturbed, or, am I normal? Have you ever wondered if you are a psycho? Have you ever wondered if you are on the way to losing it? I do. I have. I am now wondering. I do not talk about it - that is - if I had somebody to talk about it with - but it is there for me, the questions. What am I afraid of? Why am I afraid that others will discover my sense of hopelessness? Because they will recommend 'I see somebody', translated to mean a Psychiatrist, and I do not want to see a Psychiatrist who will just try to make me a little less hopeless. But what is there to be hopeful for. Am I hopeful for the diseases in the world, or, the human inhumanity in the world, or, the way there is always tragedy, or the way the ordinary person has to constantly struggle to stay ahead of the curve when it is impossible to stay ahead of the curve.

Being isolated, alone, feeling hopeless, there are millions of others, billions who feel the same way. Some of these try to rectify the feelings by joining a religion or a cult or getting together with others, always being with others, participating, and it does seem to work for them, but I just cannot seem to work up the feeling. I just seem to love swimming in my own sense of hopelessness; it is there, and I embrace it and while I embrace it, I suffer for it, and while I suffer for it, I feel sorry for myself suffering for it. It is a cycle that I am in that I enjoy being in and hate being in. Fascinating.

Time, today, feeling no energy to do anything, no energy to even leave my house, to go to the local supermarket, to do anything, time, today, plenty of it before the house is filled tonight, time on my hands. Time, measuring myself, wondering about myself as usual, trying to set a plan for my future in action, or, at least in my head. But there is no plan, no action. I feel devoid of ideas, devoid of vision. That is scary. I have never been devoid of vision before; I have always had a plan and confidence I could succeed in carrying it out. I always had an idea that I was going to succeed, triumph over odds, triumph as a writer and even as a humanitarian, but those ideas seem to be buried somewhere now. I have no plan and no ideas about success.

I feel like I am treading water and that will be my plight over the rest of my life. And while these ideas swill through my head, I visualize others I knew in the past, visualize their success as opposed to my failures. Others, those I studied with who are now full professors, others I worked with and are now top executives earning big money, others, who have made it, who have earned it, who are happy and contented, who are not isolated, who do not despair, who are not hopeless. I envy these others, I hate these others, and I hate myself. I hate everything and everyone.

Help, I am falling apart, I can see that before my eyes. I wish I could pull the covers over my head and just wish it all away. Is this classic depression? Is it classic unemployment? These are questions I have. I do know that I need help, somebody, anybody to give me a sense of direction, to give me wisdom. I am looking for help, but no longer know how to ask for help. I am isolated in my own mind, which is the worst place to be isolated. I cannot reach out, don't know how to reach out. This is something that has been coming on me a long time. Even at the last job, the problem with the last job was I no longer knew how to ask for help to deal with the job and the boredom of the job.

Is it a loss of faith in my fellow man that has done this to me? Another question, yes. I fear asking for help because I fear the answers my fellow humans will give me. Their answers always seem too complicated, complicating matters; their answers always seem too naïve, to unworkable. Their answers always seem to present me with more questions than answers. That's why I fear asking them anything, asking for help. I also may be afraid of their judgment. Human beings can be judgmental and I do not ever want to be judged or be treated like I am on trial in any shape or form.

Asking for help also gets you involved and often times I have found myself not wanting to get involved. Asking for help obliges you to others and when you are obliged to them, you must listen to them, obey them, being at their command, you must be able and prepared to do their bidding. The thought of this turns my stomach. Why would I ever want to be obliged to others, why would I ever want to be drawn into their complex world or worlds? I want to just mind my business and walk above things. That is my goal. That is my dilemma. Walking above things is alienating myself from things, and alienating myself means depressing myself, which ultimately means creating the hopelessness of things. I know. It's true. But I cannot turn things around myself. I need help that I cannot ask for.

A bad situation. Walls are everywhere and there are now tools to lay siege to the walls and liberate the city.

Unalterable.

AUGUST 2001

# WEEK 1

## Wednesday, August 1, 2001

A new attempt on my part to raise myself out of the unalterable despair I am beginning to fall into. It is August now, a new month, thirty or thirty one new days (how many days does August have?) and I must get my act together. I have sent out resumes so you never know what might occur. I sit by the phone and wait, but nobody calls for me; they call for my wife; she has been applying for jobs too, wanting to leave her teaching position for a better position in school administration, supervision, that is, being a school supervisor or assistant principal or director or principal of directors, etc. She has been getting calls, she has been interviewing for those jobs, while I sit like a baked potato in the suburbs wondering how a forty-eight year old man has descended into a position so low that I cannot seem to work myself out of it.

Jealous, that has entered into my mind set now, jealous at my wife, the real supporter of the family. Me, an out of work writer in the computer industry, a writer of fiction as well and philosophy as well who could never rise above the ranks of the rank amateur, me, the failure, watching my wife be a success. Jealousy eating up my insides, torturing me. Jealousy, we've talked about that before and here it is again. I sometimes believe that it is this trait in me that has brought me down to these depths, that has ruined any chance of success I have in my career or careers. Jealousy is the green eyed monster, or, just the monster.

Jealousy always makes you feel deprived even when you are not. Jealousy makes the rich man feel poor and wanting more, much more to compete with his much richer neighbors. Jealousy makes you distrustful of those around you who become your competitors. Jealousy makes you not appreciate what you have or what you could have. There is always that feeling of being denied, that the world, God, man is playing a trick on you to deny you, always that feeling of ruination.

Spoiled, jealousy has spoiled everything for me. Taking any sense of triumph and turned it into tragedy. Worse, it has made me bitter against my fellow man for having more than me, being happier than me. On the surface, jealousy is good, it provides the fuel, the energy, it is a driving force, a competitive force to make you excel, do better than your neighbor, on the surface, but in the long run, it detracts, holds you back, curtails your innate drive, curtains your ambition, makes your lifeless, makes you bitter, and ultimately, completely ruins you. I know. I have been a jealous man, an envious man and now I pay the price for it.

My wife, she will soon have a great job, a better job than I could ever have and it is now time for me to drop the jealousy, to reverse the trends of my life. Is it ever too late? Can I turn around my life? Let me start by being happy for my wife, let me start by trying to be happy for the accomplishments of others. Why shouldn't other people succeed, be happy, and be healthy and wealthy? Are they not entitled to that! By rooting for them, not being jealous of them, by taking pride in their accomplishments, will I not be growing? Maybe that is the key. I will start with my wife and then see. I already am feeling better.

Thoughts away from myself that is a good thing, thinking of others, concentrating on their wants and desires, their happiness, this is good. Growing up and concentrating on the self, being selfish, can be very hard when taken to the extreme, I can see that now. Living the life of SELF, every minute of every day is weighed, every second is questioned, and, what type of life is that anyway, what type of enjoyment can be gained in that. Sit back, watch and enjoy others as they live life, marvel at their pursuits, dreams, accomplishments. Push the SELF, ambitions, jealousies, into the background, and just live life. That seems so much easier, and, I think, in the end, you, I can accomplish more myself. When I marvel at others, I can freely do for myself without any preconceptions, any barriers. I free my body and soul up for life ahead and can act freely. Barriers go away. Feelings of competition go away.

Freedom, have I discovered it. I don't know yet.

### Thursday, August 2, 2001

Rethinking my thoughts of yesterday while trying to deal with my son's neurosis. He hates his new day camp, hates the counselors, the camp, the activities, says there is a bully in the bunch, complains about the lunches, but, still, my wife and I have made him return today; the money for the camp is long spent and we are bound and determined he will continue there for the two weeks.

We cannot let my son be a quitter. A quitter isn't the American way. We are fighters, fighting through all odds, all problems, heading towards the ultimate victory of victories. Isn't this correct? I have my doubts, to be honest. Going ahead, bulling ahead is fine when you are on the right course, of course it is right when you are on the right course, but what happens when you are on the wrong course, or an evil course, or a course that leads to your own downfall and doom? I ask this question and speak from personal experience. When I was younger and supposedly much stupider (although, I would say that I am as much of a fool today), I met a girl that was wrong for me, I knew she was wrong for me, we didn't get along that well, our families didn't get along that well, but I bulled ahead with her, out of fear of being alone or whatever, and we got married because I pushed, and then we promptly got divorced, promptly and then I looked around and didn't understand. My studies, history, liberal arts, studying, bullying ahead without thought, without any thought to the future, without any thought of applying my studies, bullying ahead and in the end having nothing to show for it. Also, bullying ahead with a philosophy of life, a view of life of a cynical nature, a view that proved to be wrong often times but one in which I continued and continued and continued to use and absurd and which continued to lead me towards the wrong conclusions. Bulling, moving forward in our convictions without ever examining those convictions, moving ahead with our prejudices without examining them, the idea always being to move ahead, to bull ahead. That is the problem with most of us, to be honest; we believe in progress for progress sake and never analyze where the progress is taking us or how deadly each step in the progression is.

This is the message I am giving my son, bull your way through, never quit with an idea or an action. Be a man, be brave and strong and true blue and you will see you will triumph in the end. What a lie! What a crock of crap. Why am I teaching him this? Maybe because that is the American way, the way of our fathers and I am too weak to stop the process, maybe, also because this is my wife's way and my wife rules this domicile, especially now with me being out of work and out of chances. Bull, move ahead, progress, a laugh if there ever was one.

Rethinking my philosophy, trying to be less jealous, less judgmental, less selfish and more selfless, trying. What was I thinking yesterday? I don't know if I know how to be like that without sacrificing myself completely. That's what scares me, sacrificing myself completely, obliterating myself before I even begin. Being selfless, is that really good? Don't you have to look after yourself first, number one, before you can look after others? I've heard that. Maybe it isn't bad being a selfish bastard, jealous of all around me. I don't know. I have no idea anymore. That's part of my problem now; I do not have any of the answers. I see answers but no solutions; I see answers but without questions; I see answers with counter-answers. Where to turn for the correct answers? Where to turn.

It is utterly confusing know what is right, what is wrong. As a result, I sit on the fence, always on the fence, one of my recurring life themes, sitting there on the fence and not being able to choose the right answers. This afflicts other people as well, I am sure; here again is another reason they choose religion; religion guarantees them the right answers to life. The Gospels, the Talmud, the Hadith, guarantees of wisdom, guarantees of the right answers. Everybody wants the right answers, everybody wants to be sure. Religion as an alternative; embracing it to lead me to the conclusions. I have doubts because I have seen so many of the religious bent who have no answers at all and are as confused as you or me. How scary is that. Think about it. Think of the magnitude of it, that is, there are no right answers out there, or at least, no certain answers. So what do I conclude: we are all just guessing at things, choosing this answer or that in the hopes that it is the right one, hoping, praying it is the right one but never knowing for sure, although pretending to be sure?

I cannot pretend anymore. There are all these answers and one is as good as the other for all I can tell. I cannot choose.

I cannot!

## Friday, August 3, 2001

Watching television news, listening to the commentators who discuss the state of the economy, I make several observations and they are not good ones. These idiots, these visions on screen, these images on my screen, mostly middle aged newsmen, young and bouncy blonde newswomen, most, have no idea of what they're saying or why they're saying it. Nor, do the people that they are interviewing, government and business leaders who talk in deep authoritative voices but whose eyes of uncertainty give them away for the fools they are. I watch, we all watch expecting, hoping for real information; what you basically get is nothing, words, audio sounds, that hit your ears but provide nothing else except a temporary sensation to the senses.

They, those on the television and in authority everywhere, they tell me about the economy, they make their predictions, but they do not know, they guess and frame their guesses in absolutes. It is all part of the game, searching for the concrete, the definitive. What we should understand instead is that all of us human beings are really monkeys; when you listen to commentators, Presidents, Prime Ministers, Business Leaders, etc., etc., etc., and the list goes on and on and on, you must remember that you are listening to monkeys like yourself, people all who live in caves like yourself and have the basic needs like yourself. There is little special about them, these monkeys except they may have more material possessions then yourself and have access to mass media devices. Why do I watch and listen to them, then? Boredom, it is something to do, pass the time, pass the life, but always with hope that they have something intelligible to say that will change your life.

I am always waiting for that event that will change my life that is the truth about my life. I am always waiting for that one momentous event that will not just change my life but bring it to a sense of fulfillment, to Nirvana, to the highest form of art so to speak. This is the sad part of course, very sad since you spend your existence waiting for something that never occurs. I am always waiting, and if not waiting for the actual event, waiting for a sign of the coming of the actual event, almost like waiting for signs of the Messiah coming or returning to Earth.

Will the event come? I have almost come to the conclusion that this great event will never come, that this is a product of my stupid imagination. Living for a moment that I imagine will raise my life to some higher level, stupid, foolish, blind, and many more words I cannot think of at this point. Being a writer, an artist, a man of belles' letters or just my P's and Q's, I have thought of that moment as one of discovery. Some publisher will discover me, the public will discover me, people will discover me and my novels and my essays and I will be famous and I will be on television and on the radio and books will be written about me and I will be able to go to any bookstore in the world and find my books. That moment, a discovery, here I am world, yes, you can have my autograph. Waiting for the moment so that moment can tickle my ego. It is all a matter of ego and self-love. I know I am wrong, have been wrong. I know, at least theoretically, that I should live for each moment, not wait for anything, enjoy what I have when I have it and never be deluded with delusional thoughts. I cannot help it. My mind, my ego, is waiting for that moment, that one break, that one event that will turn everything around, bring about a personal paradise.

Are there others who live for an imaginary moment in time, a future event that will turn things around? Of course, that I do know. Religious people of all stripes are waiting for that moment in time; they are waiting for that person, that Messiah. Yes, they live for Him, in him, for him, speculate about what he will do, how he will do it, religious people can live for the moment like I do. There are others too, the secular ones, they live for the moment, they wait for the opportunity to make the money that will make their fortune, they wait for that moment, that sign that will change their luck, they wait for the instant when an event will make their family life better, their job prospects better, they look for that medicine or that drug that will instantly bring them the joy they always wanted. Living for the moment that turns it around, it is a common ailment and ailment I know it is.

But it is an escape from the reality of the reality of life. When life is that boring or that mundane, when you are unhappy, sad, depressed, it is natural to clutch on to something that can happen in the future that will instantly make things right. The belief is a defense mechanism of sorts, protecting us from utter mental ruin, keeping us going, etc., etc., etc. But how can I continue when I know the secret, down deep I do, the secret being that there are no events out there that can make my life better or more worthy. There is nothing out there that will make sense of any of it. No one thing will ever happen to make me the successful writer; there will not be a break, a piece of luck, a chance meeting that will lead to other chance meetings. I know this, down deep I do and that is ultimately the problem.

Knowing is not necessarily the answer.

*WEEK 2*

## Monday, August 6, 2001

My wife, her, she, interviewing, mentioned that, incapable at this point of long sentences, early in morning, mind seems damaged, wife, interviewing, her friends calling, many friends and family to wish her well, fellow teachers calling to wish her luck, interviews, her, me, no interviews, me, unemployed, nothing doing pal, nothing doing at all.

Inability to articulate, to expand my words, not capable, depression causing depression in words and ability to express them. My wife, she is one with the world, has friends at work, is busy at home, shares with others, has joy with others. I, inarticulate, me, the words are beginning to escape me. I am not jealous of her, my wife's ability to deal with the world, her many friendships, her many teacher friends, the many other friends from elementary school and beyond that she maintains. I once had friends - at least in my twenties and thirties I did - I once was happy, was fairly well-adjusted at work, went out with friends, did things with the world, once, once I had a positive attitude toward life, once, when was that, when did I start to isolate myself, cut myself off from others, withdraw inside to my own mind? First I picked a fight with one good friend, and then another. Isolation. The same at work, not talking to co-workers, not sharing, not putting myself on the line. How long has it gone on? Ten years, since I had my son eleven years ago, since we moved to suburbia. Maybe, ten years, it has been going on for years, I do know that, isolation of self, myself, but there was no one thing that brought it about.

Practiced with isolation as a child, without friends, wandering alone, but never by choice, but it was practice nonetheless; now, isolation by choice, distancing myself from others and their opinions. And with the isolation comes the depression and with the depression comes the further isolation, and it all probably stems from my disappointment in life. I wanted to be somebody but the reality is I never did and never can and never will be. Accepting this made me pull away from people, to want to live through my own disappointment. Looking others in the face, hearing of their accomplishments only made my own failures more evident to my mind. Pulling away, driving into the heart of isolation where I could brood on my own thoughts, failures, where I can count the minutes of my own doom, my own demise, this has become the way.

Self-flagellation, this has always been my way, my true way, even as a child; I always enjoyed putting myself down, even as a kid, always enjoyed maintaining a bad self-image of myself, even as a kid. I can remember how I always put myself down, comparing myself to the other kids and finding myself lacking. I always thought their was something lacking there, that I didn't measure up, couldn't measure up, etc., etc., etc., and throughout the self put-downs I enjoyed it, bathed in my own put-downs, comforted in them. I guess I am an emotional masochist, then and now, now and then. Now, I am isolating myself from others as a put down to myself. Things tying together, in my head, ideas coming together.

One thing, people always said that I have always lacked confidence. They have said that this has presented me from achieving, they have said. It's true; I have no confidence because it's easier to have none. When you have no confidence, you do not have to do because you imagine you cannot do, and when you do not have to do, it is easier, but when it is easier, you feel more depressed, and when you feel more depressed, you want to isolate yourself, which makes it easier because then you will not have to do, which makes you depressed, and thus the cycle goes.

Not doing, not wanting to do, not having the confidence to do, maybe it all goes back to my being lazy. Numbers of people have told me that throughout my life, particularly my mother, who always said I could do anything if only I wasn't so lazy. Maybe that's where this all stems, the low self-esteem, the masochism, the desire to isolate myself, maybe it is that I am just lazy, do not want to do anything because I do not want to move myself, am lazy, seek a lazy lifestyle and the way to lead it is through self-eradication. Could be. Nice theory. Yes. Maybe. Who knows?

What I know or think I know is that a human being is only a series of experiences; therefore, what you put in, is what you are; therefore, if you put in nothing, you are nothing; if you lead a full life, participating in life, you have a full personality, are a participant, and are happy. True? Maybe? Yet, maybe I don't want to have a full life? Maybe I want to put into my life sterility and receive sterility back? Maybe I want to be the isolated hermit and have my life represent that.

Thoughts swirling about on this Monday. They are painful thoughts, worrisome thoughts, but cannot be turned off. They will doom me. I know.

### Tuesday, August 7, 2001

My son still complaining about camp, my wife still going on and on about her ambitions to be a school administrator, about her interviews, talking on the phone, my wife, telling friends and family about her ambitions and her desires, on and on, while I sit in the background downstairs, alone, trying to fathom it. The only person at peace seems to be my daughter. She likes day camp, she likes me, kisses me, asks how I am, the eight year old is asking with kindness in her voice. In this harsh world, this world of nasty dispositions and constant demands, her voice, her sweetness are like my bright shining star.

People have often heard the different tone in my voice I have when addressing my daughter. They say that I never yell at her or discipline her, that I am spoiling her. Agreed on all counts. But again, in this harsh world, where men and women are always scrambling for position from the time they are babes in the carriage, it is welcome relief to see the light and the joy and the softness, in is welcome joy to live for it, to live towards the idea of softness. To see my daughter's smile, her innocence at the world at large, to see her speak of the beauty, to watch her draw crayon pictures of trees and flowers and loved ones, what can be better in life. Yet, there are those, around and around and around you, who constantly declare that children must grow up to face the realities of life, which are often bitter. Life and death and making money and sex and obligations to parents and spouses and children and disasters both natural and unnatural, face facts that the world stinks. They always want everyone to face the facts that the world sucks and I do not understand this philosophy. Preserve childhood for as long as possible; preserve innocence for as long as possible, that to me seems appropriate. Maintain the sweet, dispose of the bitter or at least push it to the side or delay its ascendancy. That to me would seem normal but it is not considered normal.

We do not want to preserve the innocence and beauty; we rush to destroy it through economic exploitation, sexual exploitation, and emotional exploitation. It does make you laugh. We do talk about yearning for the innocence of youth and we do like to watch films and paintings and the like that preserve it, but these are only quick glimpses. The object of all is to destroy innocence, to educate the innocence out of them, to make their goal to have money and possessions, to toil, to listen to unjust family members and employers without rebellion, to stand mute while the greater authorities sculpt your life in the shape and form they desire. Destruction of innocence so that it becomes bleak.

And this objective is not a cultural one, particularly. Not at all. We find that in all cultures, progressive, backwards, the youth, the beauty, the innocence is destroyed through religion, sex, marriage, obligation, economics, etc., etc., etc. It seems the goal of humanity, to humanize the innocent and bring them into the human family of bleakness. You will find this in a tribal society or a nuclear society, it doesn't seem to matter and it makes me sick, depressed, and it makes me hold on to my daughter's innocence and try to preserve it with that much more conviction.

That's what makes me sad too, the fact that what is good and beautiful is in essence that fragile. Some how, some way, I remember the phrase, we must protect the weak from the powerful, which I guess in the traditional sense means, we must protect women and children from the evil of the world. I take it to mean more than that. Art, the environment, the rivers, the valleys, the clear blue sky, the animals, fragile, things about us that are beautiful, dear, that are not harsh, are always prone to be destroyed, killed, made bleak, and it always can be done so easily. The harshness of life is always around the corner and it is always stronger, or so it seems, and everything that brings a smile that is gentle and soft to the touch, is so brittle, so quickly destroyed. I keep this in mind every day, every hour on the day; how I have to guard against the harshness in myself, keep from destroying what is good, encourage the good, nurture the good as if they are rare houseplant seeds to be coddled into germination and beyond.

It is fearful too when you become aware of the fragility of the tender and the good around you, very fearful. You realize, I realize that I have a responsibility to encourage and promote the preservation of all that is good and tender, the sweet and the pure; I realize that everything I do and say must work towards that greater good. Yes, it is a responsibility and one that I do not take lightly. That is why I walk on eggs when dealing with other human beings, other situations, when I am so careful with my daughter and with my son, to encourage the sweet and the tender.

Darkness, it is so easy to encourage that, it being all around and the world constantly directing its attentions to ending the purity in the human heart and turning all into the bleak night. It is so easy to do and say things that destroys the aesthetic, a word, a gesture, a thought, can turn it all to rubbish, all that makes life worth living.

Fear. I am fearful. Responsibility it is mine.

## Wednesday, August 8, 2001

I am not sure what to write this morning. I am blank of ideas right now; I feel blank of life as well. It is scary to be blank, to have no idea what's up and what's down. You want to believe that you know it all, that's how you want to lead your life, confidently. But I am not confident today because I have no idea of it all and no answers to any of it.

Does anybody have answers to anything? I wonder. If they say they have answers, are they lying? I wonder. Scientists seem sure of themselves, like they have answers, but most of the world's phenomena is still unexplained. Doctors seem sure of themselves, but we still are dying of incredible diseases, and there are still new diseases turning up on a daily basis. Technology, the entire field made up of technicians and technocrats everywhere seem sure of themselves, but despite the technical innovations, there are still desperate individuals, war, terror, uncertainty and technology seems clueless to deal with any of it. We do not know, have no answers, if you want to be straight about it. Teachers do not have the answers, politicians do not have the answers, philosophers do not have the answers, religious people do not have the answers, etc., etc., etc. My favorite in the group are the religious ones; the pious ones freely admit to having no answers, freely admit that God has all the answers, but in the end say that they get the answers from God, through prayer and meditation God provides them with answers, that they are the vessels for answers from God. Interesting, but I must question the techniques used, the rituals used to get the answers from God. How do you know it is actually God speaking to you, providing you with ideas instead of your own mind kicking in, your own mind manipulating the thoughts and stamping them mistakenly with God's label? Interesting to think about. God as inspiration, God as the source of the ultimate answers? I have to question this only for one reason.

Look at the course of human activity, religious activity throughout history. God's work? Man's work? I would say that it is man's work, man pretending to have answers from God and acting for God but committing the ultimate sins, allowing for ignorance and poverty and brutality and insensitivity. If the line between God and humans is clear and there is a clear path of communication there through bibles and prayer and meditation and such, why have humans behaved as they have, why do we still lack the real answers in our lives? It is a very basic question. Sometimes people come back in defense that answers have been communicated to only a few, Jesus, Muhammad, Moses, etc., etc., etc., and these are the ones who have relayed the answers to us through prophecy. This admits that God doesn't provide the answers directly, but through intermediaries who are dead to us in this world. Thus, we then have to go and interpret the intermediary's words, looking for the answers in them. But again, the process of the human brain kicks in and again the answers obtained with certainty and applied to God may not be God's at all but human ideas given the label of God. The problems of human history indicate this to be the case.

How to deal with all or any of it, just admit that human beings do not have answers, that we are blank vessels that have no idea of where we came from or where we are going. How simple is that. Admitting we are creatures without real ideas may make us more humble, less prone to erroneous actions, actions in which we self-righteously destroy one another because we feel we are right. Admitting the idea that we have ideas may make us more humble, more peaceful, and more civilized in the end. It could also make us more bleak, more depressed, less industrious and ambitious as humans. For certain, there would be great changes. But reality is reality, and the reality is, there are no answers for human beings. God may have the answers, or Gods, or whatever you believe in - technology - may have them, but it seems perfectly obvious to me that humans have no way to access the answers. Obvious!

All this talk about answers and who has them brings up the point - at least in my head - about organized religion. I have had friends, acquaintances, co-workers, family members, ad nauseam that has been vehemently opposed to organized religions. They take every moment to crucify them, to explain their faults, to call their defenders and upholders crooks and phonies and charlatans of every sort. They take pleasure in talking about the real decadence of the organized faiths, saying that in the future the world will grow tired of them and dispossess them. I listen. I believe. I don't believe.

Organized religion is supposed to provide the real answers. We've said that already. We've also said, I have at least, that we humans do not have any answers. So what good is organized religion? That is a question I don't seem to have much answer to. In one sense, I know it is a money making venture, it provides jobs for preachers and architects; it helps create charitable organizations, which employ more people, etc. That is all well and good. And maybe it is good that there is organized religion for people to believe in, to turn to for answers. Maybe it would all be too depressing without that. People who could not find comfort may not be able to cope with this world and its puzzles and paradoxes. This is true. But, I can see where those people I have mentioned would be angry at organized religion, at overzealous priests and rabbis and ministers and imams, those who walk about self-righteously, thinking they know it all and charging for the right to speak to them about it. Everybody is entitled to get angry, angry at the religious if they want to. My feeling is, however, that it is all a waste of energy. All you have to do is realize that nobody has the answers, that they do not exist in this human world and no priest or rabbi or whatever can ever provide you with them. After you realize that, it all becomes so much simpler. You can look in the preacher's eyes, the politician's eyes, the employer's eyes, etc., with knowledge that they have no knowledge and that they are stupid humans like yourself who are all in the same boat as yourself. It makes things easier in the end.

Life is knowledge, knowledge that there is no real knowledge.


## Thursday, August 9, 2001


Isolation, my own, returning to the subject of previous days that I mentioned in previous days in this journal, my isolation, saying why I sought to be isolated. The subject keeps returning to me; I cannot get away from the thoughts, and the why of it, why would I want to isolate myself? Reasons mentioned before, masochism, not liking people, etc. Yes, and there is truth there, probably lots of it. But the more I've thought about it, a few other things have popped up or popped out or just popped. My desire for isolation, to isolate myself, to alienate myself from my own environment can also be explained by my continuing journey in life to understand self and from my continuing struggle to understand the incomprehensible loneliness.

Monks are like this, religious hermits, who move away from life as we know it, lock themselves away and then try to contemplate themselves, God, their fellow man, etc., etc., etc. They wear a certain garb, take vows of silence and poverty and then try to obtain all the wisdom they can from the experience. During this time, I imagine - though I do not know for sure - I expect they are praying for the world and its people and its morality, etc., and so forth and so on. Theirs may be a voyage of discovery, just as I think mine is. By isolating, I am turning inward to contemplate all that is still around me, discovering what is around me.  But the beauty of it is that I have not physically moved away like the monk has moved away. I am still amidst humanity, emotionally detached but physically in proximity. Thus I can turn inward and drawn on my own emotional pain but use my physical eyes and ears to attain an understanding of those around me; the physical reconnaissance done, the information gained with the eyes and ears is then taken back to my inner self, the pained self and I can put two and two together to make a number that is both even and true.

I guess when I was younger, I wanted to make that voyage of discovery through traveling and reading books, by talking to others, by physically participating, that is, having sex, drinking, going to sporting events, going to bars, listening to music, going to the latest movie and that type of nonsense. In this way, I did discover but my discoveries were limited. Following the herd, hitting on popular culture, participating in popular culture, teaches you nothing except about popular culture. You become merely the product of your age, but never get a better glimpse of more meaningful issues like life and death. I have chosen another method, the alienation of affections method, pulling myself from the emotional mud-slides of life and watching from a bunker some distance from the scene. From here, I can try to understand what it means to be alive, to live, to breathe, to have diseases, to have joy and sorrow, and from this bunker I can also try to unravel the idea of death, what does it mean, how does it feel or not feel. By isolating myself amidst life, I am in essence giving myself up to death; in fact, I am dead, a dead man walking and thus can begin to comprehend the whole process of the next world, if there is any.

Interesting this voyage. It is a voyage that costs nothing in dollars and cents and is easy to achieve. All you need to do is cut yourself off from your loved ones and the world of traditional mores and values, cut yourself off from popular values and culture and the like. That's all folks. So it is difficult, though not materially. One great difficulty is isolation yourself while apparently not isolating yourself to others. Doing it secretly, moving away emotionally without specifying what you are doing to them, to the outside world, is not easy. Isolating oneself has to be done alone and without the help or knowledge of others. The moment your secret is revealed, others will try to bring you back into the fold; the moment your desire becomes known, others may run for professionals to right your course. The moment your desire becomes known, you will be called a hermit, a fruitcake, a nut, a depressed individual, a sick individual, an individual in need to help, etc., etc., etc. So the course of isolation is a solo one and one that must be taken in secrecy, which makes it hard.

To pull yourself away from the world is also hard and takes years and years of effort to effectively get there, and it has me. The only problem is once you are isolated and living within a sealed emotional vacuum, how do you get back. I am in a deep cocoon, depressed, out of touch, how do I reconnect with the world around me? That is one of the real questions that I have for myself and I am just trying to come to grips with it. I have begun making attempts to reconnect, trying to talk to others, trying to be concerned with my wife, with my parents, with jobs; I have talked to Headhunters on the phone, shone real interest in jobs and getting them, interest, real, not imagined, but without much luck. There is this feeling of disconnection with others which I cannot shake. Maybe when I find a job? It might get worse then; my last few jobs, I was totally disconnected from those around me; all my co-workers looked at me strangely, I know that. How to get connected again. A good question.

Sometimes I think I am not really isolated, not really so alone and alienated. Maybe I am imagining it, maybe. Maybe I am dreaming? Could be.

### Friday, August 10, 2001

So I sit on Friday, another Friday, the end of the work week in the Judeo-Christian world, another one. But, a thought comes to me, is this the end of the work week to the Hindu-Muslim-Buddhist-Zoroastrian-Sikh etc., etc., etc., world? I don't think so. This end of the work week thing is specific to the Jews and Christians. I wonder if the Jews and Christians living amongst the others, in the others' lands, I wonder if Friday is still there end of the work week. Probably not. But does it matter. Probably not. But at least it gives me something to think about right now. Right now, I want to think a lot about things that don't matter. It is going to be my therapy.

Have you ever done that, forced yourself to think about things that don't matter, things that do not effect life and death like sports, for example, or collecting baseball cards, for example, or playing chess, for example. Therapy, it is good, passes the time, thoughts that do not effect life or death, they are good thoughts, or can be just so long as they do not lead you to the darker ideas of life. Therapy, thinking of lighter things, not always the darker things. Thinking of the darker things can reduce life to one dark tunnel. I have been there, done that. I had a friend some years back who thought only of himself, of his life, of his death, of the death of his friends and family, only of health and lack of health leading to death. Not married, never married, without kids, he'd wander through life with the dark cloud above, work at his job with the dark cloud, walk about the world with that dark cloud, deal with others with that dark cloud. There could be joy in a room but once he entered, there could only be doom. I as the friend, tried to be cheery, tried to get the individual to focus on mindless things not effecting life and death, dating the opposite sex, listening to music, playing an instrument and producing music, playing chess, going to the movies, but through it all, through everything ideas of death flooded in. Music, his father liked music, his dead father who never enjoyed life during life; women, dating them, couldn't because they reminded him of his dead mother, a woman who never lived, couldn't live, was too nervous to live. Ideas, of life and death and that cloud hanging over his head. He is an ex-friend now; I couldn't deal with my life becoming his shroud.

So I am trying to force my mind - during this period of unemployment - towards other things. So I have tried to concentrate on my gardening hobby. I grow succulents and cactus and some other houseplants, I plant rare seed and nurture them towards germination, and I succeed a lot. It takes time, digging in the dirt, planting, fertilizing, repotting, placing and un-placing plants throughout the house and backyard, time not spent in thought of myself or impending doom or current alienation. I pick up newspapers and read the current events. I listen to the radio and current affairs and talk programs. I take a walk or a brief drive to nowhere. I do, moving my mind away from the darkness, and succeed occasionally, but the ideas, no money, lack of money, leading to lack of basic essentials, leading to thoughts of my children having no basic essentials, leading to thoughts of losing the house, leading to thoughts of death and destruction, come back home to my mind of minds. And being here alone, in the suburbs with others gone to work, alone, isolated, fearing isolation brings those thoughts of life and death back, it saps me of all energy to do other things, gardening, listening to radios, reading newspapers. Dark thoughts flooding in like tidal waves from Japan hitting the shores of Western Civilization. No where to go, no where to turn, to turn off the ideas and thoughts.

There are times you want to just be mindless, to think nothing and just sit there like the cow in the pasture, but it is a hard thing to do when alienation is there and it keeps pulling at your lapels. When I think of wanting to be mindless, that is thinking of only mindless things that do not concern life and death issues, I think of my late grandmother who passed away at ninety-five. She was in a nursing home those last years, apparently senile, but she seemed happy, few thoughts, few worries. You gave her a hard sucking candy and there was that smile on her face and this sense of peace. Others looked at her with pity, I with envy. If only we could all be so freed of thoughts, thoughts of life and death. Trouble with most of us, we take things too seriously, look at our own lives too seriously, our husbands/wives, children, aunt, uncles, co-workers, too seriously. Maybe we are just searching for some relevance in our own lives and in this search, we make things bigger than they are, make simple things into grave thoughts and then the complications begin and then life becomes a great anchor taking you down.

Life shouldn't be that tedious or that heavy; life should be simple, and if it is not maybe there is something wrong with you, with me, maybe we both are complicating it too much with details thoughts of gloom and doom. Maybe these thoughts of unemployment are not necessary. Maybe I should just grab a sandwich and a cold soda, eat and enjoy. Possible. Possibilities. They                                                                     exist.

# WEEK 3

## Monday, August 13, 2001

Monday, rolling around again, around and around, time passing and Monday rolling around. And as always, I am circling the want ads, sending out the emails, searching the Internet for jobs, but always feeling it would do no good.

That is the phrase, always thinking it would 'do no good.' I have no hope, not really. I know down deep that even if I get a job - which right now is not so clear - it will be one that is evil smelling, stupid, boring, and that the people that I will be working for will be: stupid, nasty, evil, rapacious, pernicious, parsimonious, and vengeful. I have to be honest, don't I? I'm forty-eight years old and in the business I found myself these past twenty some odd years, the computer field, forty-eight is very, very old, almost ancient. In this last job, where they showed me the back of the metal door on the way out, I was the oldest, older by many years than the head of the company. Employees were mostly in their early or late twenties, possibly their thirties, and one closing in on forty. So there I was, standing out in a field where I could easily be a grandfather. Few wish to hire somebody like me, a writer in the computer field, at my age. Those that want me, want me to work only for a month or two as a consultant, maybe three months at most. Age is a matter of mind, but in the practical world, age is not in the mind, it is in the paycheck or the lack of a paycheck.

I should try to take it from the employer's point of view. He sees somebody at my age, with my experience and immediately thinks: 'high priced.' Then, he/she thinks, why pay more when you can get somebody cheaper, somebody younger and cheaper who can do the same thing. And the truth is, most of these white collar jobs, one can replace another, one person can push paper and hit a computer key like another. Experience is not a factor except in the deluded mind of the public at large. It is a myth, this idea of experience for most jobs. Most jobs are trivial, needing little of the mind, little of the experience. Pick up papers, typing a report, putting together some spreadsheet, cleaning floors, etc., etc., etc., most jobs have little meaning and need little skill. It is not true for all, effective teachers and doctors, carpenters, plumbers, there is skill and experience does count. But for the great majority who do not fall into these categories, it makes no difference at all; employers with big bad corporations have their pick. Go for the cheapest, is very smart indeed.

Another reason to go for a younger kid out of school then the experienced fool with years in the business, any business, molding, brainwashing, etc., etc., etc., is always easiest to accomplish with a younger fool rather than an older fool. They, the employer knows this; get a kid, develop a company man/woman with a company mentality. Once they are part of the company, with the company tattooed on their chest, you can get more work out of them, pay them less and generally push and abuse them a little further. This doesn't mean that they feel obliged to take care of their new company man or woman forever; in fact, at the first sign of fiscal crisis, the company man or woman will find themselves out on the narrow streets of the world without a dime in their pockets and wondering why and what. What went wrong for them? How could the employer do this to them, they were so devoted, so loyal, they worked so hard. Confusion for the company man or woman, who never realized that they were mere chattel to be used and abused in the process.

I would hire young people too if I were the employer. They are naïve, are willing to devote their souls, lack families so they can be worked long hours and paid a little less for their devotion. I have seen this, would probably do this myself if I were in that situation. Funny part, I have seen young people out of school with their first jobs, worked with them, and have tried to warm them not to devote their souls to the company, not to be a corporate employee, not to bring the company, the product line or lines into their hearts, I have warned and instructed and all I have gotten is looks back like I was some young fool in need of electric shock therapy. The problem with talking from experience is that experience is not really looked upon that wonderfully in this technologically based society where things, technical things and other things, change moment to moment. In other words, to have experience means you are dated, and to be dated means you are out of touch and to be out of touch means you are old and ready for the waste bin.

I've seen that in the computer field. The more you know, the less marketable you will be in the future. That is because what you know becomes real old, real quick. Technology is not some fine art or some real craft like plumbing or hair cutting. It is passing. The only way to stay in touch, not get old is to keep studying the new and the yet to be produced, the new software, the new hardware, constantly studying, learning, always, never stopping, because the moment you stop studying is the moment you are old and ready for the dust bin of time, like, I am ready for the dust bin of time.

It is all so funny and sad. And the saddest note of all is how human have become merely components in some sort of whirlwind, not beings in themselves that have importance, but cogs in a network of some high governmental-business sort, cogs that can be replaced, cogs without faces and names. These are the same cogs that were namely and faceless in the machine age with its industrial revolutions and automation revolutions, namely and faceless. There is nothing as fearsome as that. Human beings drowned in a sea of nuts and bolts, human beings drowned but continuing to survive.

Sad and worrisome. Yes.

## Tuesday, August 14, 2001

My wife's last day of Summer School teaching is today and my kids finish summer camp the middle of next week or something like that. I cannot keep up with my family anymore; I cannot keep all the detail in check. Details seem to run together. What people tell me seems to run together. My wife, she tells me about dates, times, people we will be meeting, things will be doing, but I don't hear, cannot hear. I don't seem to hold any importance in dates and times. The only dates and times that come to mind are the dates and times in my past that I have had operations, medical ones, as a teenager having a hernia operation, as an adult having a cyst operation - removing a huge cyst from my ass. I remember those dates and times well, remember going to the doctors, going to the hospitals, being raped by doctors and nurseries, being reassured by doctors and nurses and various other official-sterile personnel, and then returning home with the physical pain and more reassurances of recovery. Those dates and times, I remember very well, but I have trouble remembering any other. After a time, other dates and time seem to merge together into clouds of unwavering smoke; what does it matter, Columbus Day, October 12th, off from school, off from work, going to a picnic, go to visit my sister, go to the museum, go, October 12th, holiday, Labor Day, Memorial Day, date and time; my wife, dates and times, highlighted times, passing times, everything passing and I cannot get a grip except on those dates where my body was cut open and things removed and sown up. Everything else is a blur, which is funny since I am a supposed historian who studied dates and times in school.

Historically speaking, dates and times of an impersonal nature, have always been easy for me, 1492 - Spanish Inquisition; 1096 Norman Invasion of Britain and the First Great Crusade for Christianity and the destruction of all non-believers; 1453, the conquest of Constantinople by the Turks from the Christians. I can go on with the dates here, the times here, but I will not bore you further with any of that. But why is it that I can remember the impersonal dates and not remember the personal ones. Maybe I value the impersonal ones more; see these dates as important because they are dates on which human beings died and struggled and succeeded and were happy and were sad and cried and laughed, dates of happening to my fellow man (who I cannot stand by the way, which you already knew). Personal dates, dates that really only pertain to me, what difference do they make. If I go to a party on March 22$^{nd}$, what difference does that make? Dates and times have no real relevance. I will obey them because my wife, my family, the employers out there want me to obey them, but in reality, I hold them as non-sacred topics that effect nothing over the course of time.

All of which brings me to the moving of one grain of salt, which in predominant social theory is said to be important. Some religions believe every single act and thought is essential to the world or the world as we know it. The moving of one grain of sand effects the grains of sand next to it, which affects other grains of sand, etc., ad nausea. So what one human does or thinks effects all human beings. I cannot be that sure. I cannot be that positive. I cannot believe. I do not want to believe. If your neighbor over there, next door, that annoying neighbor goes to work, is sick, says he hates himself, another race of people, if he makes his dinner engagement at eight or not, or goes to work on time or not, or takes his vacation or not, does it make a difference. In a larger view, does any human action make a difference in the larger view of views, counting the years in the thousands and the millions? What difference does human activity make? The world, the universe, all universes and solar systems and whatever astronomy tells us, goes on with or without us. Whether I, he, she, it, meets their deadlines, keeps appointments, works, dies, matters little. Is that what you might call a nihilistic viewpoint? Absolutely and I am proud of it. Being nihilistic keeps everything in perspective for me, it dulls the alienation, and the jealousy and that particular sense that life is passing me by. How can life pass me by when all of our individual actions and accomplishments don't mean much in the grand scheme of things? Whether you get that promotion at work or not means nothing to future generations or generations of other species yet to be invented by God or nature or haphazard experience. Whatever you do, it is no consequence in ten thousand years time. Human beings are constrained by being human, by being a species of animal and not immortal and all powerful. Therefore, actions of humans are not important and individual acts of individual humans are even less important.

But we shouldn't say this too loudly. Whenever nihilism in thought and action takes over control of the human being, depression sets in and with depression, humans stop doing the daily things that keep us temporarily going as human beings. We lose the reason for doing. That is why when I see others who believe in themselves, in humans, in individual actions, I say nothing. There is such a thing as the body politic and it runs on an anti-nihilistic, optimistic approach. I nod to it, smile to myself, but never try to dent the edifice. It just came to my mind that one of the reasons for the recurring theme of unemployment, changing of jobs, etc., might be due to this nihilistic attitude on my part. Jobs, the job itself, I can never believe in, devote myself to, play the game with, play the employer's game since I do not believe in it, can never believe in it, think it is all a silly mess invented by individuals in self-delusional regression towards the womb of idiocy.

Does it all matter? Not to me. But I will keep it a secret between you and me.

### Wednesday, August 15, 2001

My mind, it keeps going back to the ideas of yesterday, ideas of nihilism and me being a nihilist. I'm not even sure of the meaning of that word but I do believe it applies to me anyway, me, a person who does believe in the inherent worth of anything, that no event or event is that important, me, who believes that ultimately humans are doomed or at least some passing phase and no matter how you shape it, or what we do to shape it, there is no changing the facts of the matter, or, of the matter of facts.

How do I deal with this fact about myself when I have to live in the world where nihilism is not an accepted approach? How do I deal with the world when I hold its institutions and people up to contempt? The trouble is, I am no revolutionary, do not wish to change the world, do not wish to make it better or worse, in fact, I want to have as little to do with it as possible. This makes for a terrible dilemma. How do you look your friends, family and neighbors in the eye when you don't believe in them or do not believe in their daily lives, when you do not care about their daily lives or your own daily life? How do you work at a job when you look at jobs as silly things where silly acts are performed that never amount to anything? It is almost impossible. In the end, you are forced to become a hypocrite. So in one sense, you go out in the world with a smile, participate in daily activities with a smile, but secretly think the people you are dealing with and the activities you are engaging in are crocks of dung left to dry under a midday desert sky. Example, there I sit with my son at the kitchen table and I am helping him do his social studies homework. What makes me laugh is I am trying to tell him about the importance of both social and studies, about the importance of history and facts, about the importance of doing things right, importance about doing. Yes, it is funny since I do not believe down deep that it is important, that there can be any importance in social studies, or math or science or English or any of these subjects. It's all ridiculous. And what use will my son have for the information looking ahead into the big, bold future? He will use it to become a white collar worker (no, no, no), a blue collar worker, a lawyer (no, no, no), a dentist, a doctor, an insurance adjuster, a government functionary, a teacher, etc, etc., etc., that's what he will use this education for; he will become a professional, which translates to meaningless fool with money in pocket. Big deal. Any of the professions, helping or otherwise, big deal. Yes, my son will gain education and use it to gain a meaningless job, to gain meaningless money, to gain a meaningless wife or wives and meaningless children; he will gain the meaningless job to pay for hospitals to fix his meaningless physical existence; he will gain the meaningless job to pay for his meaningless funeral and grave marker. But there I sit, pretending enthusiasm because the world expects the enthusiasm. How sick is this. How many people play the same game, I wonder. I'm sure there are many who believe all their worldly actions are foolish but pretend to be wholeheartedly behind them. I've worked for people who on the one hand have said that their job, the company, everything relating to their employment was a crock of excrement in a jar, but on the other hand, did everything to maintain their position, even ruin others. I have seen this tendency, people don't care for their wife and children, do not believe in them, the institutions behind them, but on the other hand do every thing they can to preserve them.

This is part of the natural hypocrisy of man, it must be, has to be. Or, maybe humans are just creatures of actions, who perform actions for actions' sake. Humans existing just to perform, just to do without thought of what they are doing, or, without belief in what they are doing. It probably is not a pre-condition that anyone believes in what they are doing while they are doing it. Probably most people just don't think about it or question it like I think about it and question it. Then, again, maybe my views, my nihilist tendencies, my belief in no principle, no event, nobody, no institution, is simply a matter of a depression brought on by unemployment. This is always possible. I am depressed and that is why I am thinking like this, possible but not probably. I think many of my problems in the world start and end with me and my attitude, my tendency not to see value in things, to get bored with those things and finally to turn away from things. I have turned away from jobs? I have turned away from friends. Will I ultimately turn away from wife and children? This is a real possibility. Should I worry? No. Does it matter!!!!!!!!!!!!!

## Thursday, August 16, 2001

Wife's home now for a few weeks before she starts teaching again in September. How do I feel about it? Rather be alone, rather not to have to face her on a daily basis, not face the one who is supporting me. It is easier to deal with shame when you are alone. It is similar to feeling lonelier within a crowd then without a crowd. Walking amidst others when you are lonely is a horrible feeling; walking amidst others who are eating while you are starving is terrible. Now you get the point. Therefore, sometimes it is better to be alone, away from others of your species.

But I am still basically alone because my wife doesn't remain in the house, not for more than a minute or two at a time. She is out shopping, going to the gym, interviewing a third time for an important administrative school job somewhere, back out shopping, on the phone upstairs talking for hours, going out to dinner with teacher friends, while I remain here, by myself, with my own mind. Is it healthy being alone with your own mind? I grew up with no friends, and relied on my own mind and my own thoughts. Better? Is it better to think internally then to discuss externally with others, to share ideas with others? Interesting question. Self-exploration can allow you to see human weakness, human egotism, human heroism; external discussion with others, sharing of thoughts across the plane of Homo sapiens can bring cross pollination of ideas, but all ideas always lead back to the original idea anyway, so what is being accomplished anyway. Also, bring humans together and there is always the possibility of war and man's inhumanity to man. Can I or anybody exist in a vacuum? A vacuum can be good, like a cocoon protecting from the outside world, although the vacuum contains no air so every so often you must leave it and breathe the vapors that are external and deal with the world's human children and listen to their

words but forget their meanings. This is the price paid for
existing in the vacuum.

Watching my wife a little more closely, that is, when I
can get a glimpse of her entering and then leaving the house
continuously, I focus in on her gait. There is that utter confidence
there, that sureness, that sense of purpose. She is self-righteous
too, meaning, that she believes that whatever she does, it is
beyond repute or beyond ill repute if you like. What a contrast to
myself; I am never sure whether what I think and what I do are
right; in fact, I often question my own intentions. That is a big
part of myself and another reason the world and myself don't get
along too well. You may wish to label my syndrome as neurotic
and I must agree. While my wife views the world in a positive
light, sure that things will eventually work out, I am as sure that
things will never work out in this dark world of ours. I see the
impending doom beyond the immediate windows of my room.
My wife sees only rainbows over which are draped possibilities. I
only see rainbows as reflections of vapor that will soon disappear
into the burning son. Poetry in motion.

The difference in perspective is attributable to issues of
upbringing. My wife's major influence was parents of European
backgrounds who saw the world as one you can advance in and
within. My major influence was a father of Middle East
background who saw the world as a place where others were out
to get you, others were envious, a world of ill-luck, where even
God Almighty (Allah) played tricks on you and eventually
brought you down. Why bother with anything when you would
die anymore? What was the point of everything when it would
turn to dust anyway? Made sense to me. But now I can see how
things are put in motion, from upbringing to adulthood, attitudes
travel far, mine did.

The world is what you make of it, and I guess that is true.
My wife has a rosy view of the world and its people. She assumes
people will act right, decently, that people will care and they
seem to care for her. She's happy, has many friends, has a career
in gear, and has the affection of many more. She has a past that
she keeps in touch with, friends, school friends, child playground

friends, and firmly knows who will be her friends in the future. She's set. She's made her world into something pleasant, decorated with all these nice ribbons and bows. I admire her world; enjoy looking in because it breaks the blackness of my day.

Work and my wife, myself and work, the duality of views. When I approach a job, I see my co-workers and bosses as potential evils, laying in wait to pile on me, to ruin me, to humiliate me and show that I know nothing (which is probably true). When my wife approaches a job, she sees nice co-workers, bosses as potential helpers, work that is challenging, work that she can and will do, etc., etc., etc. What a difference a day makes or an attitude makes. It would be fascinating to behold if it wasn't my life that is currently under discussion. Who is right and wrong in this matter? Is it better to think like myself or like my wife? Think like my wife and it does become easier to live in the world, to make that career, to make that money; you also will be a happier person. Live like me, think like me, and definitely, you will not be a happier person; you will be a sadder person, a person always looking for work, for a career, etc., etc., etc. Does this make my attitudes wrong or right? I believe my position is right but that my wife, others like her, cross-sections of humanity have an absolute right to their beliefs. I, and those like me, have no right to impose our negative viewpoint on them, those with the positive viewpoint. There is room in this world for differing viewpoints, the gloomy and the positive. Equally, the positive should never be imposed on the negative, unless the negative is cancerous, meaning dangerous, meaning violent and sinister.

My world view may be negative, shrouded in darkness, disease, doom, filled with humans having a perverse nature, seeking only other people's ultimate demise, yet, this viewpoint is benign, meaning, it does not oblige me to go out there and rectify the world, try to manipulate it mentally and physically to my liking; it is not meant to use violence as the source of its inspiration. This is pure nihilism. Why try to violently change the world or change it in any way when it doesn't matter in the long run, as all will fade in the long run anyway. The dangerous ones are those whose vision falls between the positive and negative world views. These are people who see the negative, but believe it can be changed into an ultimately positive image of their own liking. These are the people that are behind the ideologies, the revolutions, the fanatical new religions. These are the ones who might plant bombs at the nearest bus terminal, these are they, those who live in a purgatory, who are negative, believing the current world is a shame, but positive too in their vision that the world can be made positive if only their steps are followed rote. I thank the Lord or whoever that I am not and never was and never can be one of these types; they are dangerous, destructive, respecting nobody, not even themselves.

To conclude this dissertation of dissertation, I am a negative person to be sure, but one who admires the positive person, the builder of the world of worlds. While I am cock-sure of my own viewpoint, why should I dose the enthusiasm of others? Belief is a personal thing. Ultimately, it makes no difference one way or another. In the end, it all comes out in the wash.

### Friday, August 17, 2001

The wife's home again today, kids are in camp again today, again and again and again. I am getting sick of using the word again. Again means repetition and repetition means boredom. I get bored a lot and I always have. I think most people get bored. Other people step in and try to fill the time of bored people and try to make money off the bored people. They do this by making movies and making television shows, and making computers and video games and theme parks and creating tourist attractions out of nothing. Fill the time; make people forget the repetition in their lives and the accompanying boredom.

We are bored as a race. The more free time we have, the more repetition there seems to be, the more bored we become. Sometimes, you try to break the boredom with drugs, with drink, with sex, even with crime, breaking the boredom. There are many ways to try. The best way - it seems to this disgruntled mind - to keep the boredom far from your shores is through acts of manual labor, working with the hands, working in the field, playing sports; when the body is occupied, the mind of thoughts moves into the background and the less thoughts, the less the boredom. All of this comes back somehow to the theme of the decadency of Western Civilization and how the industrial and then the technological revolutions have caused us to have all of this free time on our hands, which has subsequently caused humans to go nuts, that is, humans to get bored, act out, teenagers to act out, adults to act out, crime to rise, etc., etc., etc. And maybe that's the case, but too often Western Civilization is blamed for everything. What exactly is Western Civilization anyway? Why should I blame something that is merely a concept, a thought in the head of some distant intellectual? Why? I rather just look at the particulars of the situation which pertain to the word: AGAIN, meaning doing it again, repeating what you have done in the past, again and again and again. People find ways around this, repetition again and again, the sameness, the boredom, free time and boredom. People manage to fill their free time with their hobbies, with their vices, with their casual entertainments, etc. My problem with all of that is that I have the time, there is the repetition to deal with, the AGAIN to deal with, but I cannot seem to fill it. Television bores me, movies bore me, the radio most often bores me, the newspapers and magazines bore me, the computer Internet bores me, sports bores me, hobbies in general bore me, and so you see the problem. There is the free time on the one hand, and the AGAIN to deal with, repeating actions throughout the day, day after day, life traveling at a snail's pace, and then nothing to fill the time. My life lacks fillers, and not the food kind like potato and bread (fillers in the food world). What do you do in that case? How do you handle the excess time when there are no interests. Do you just sit there and contemplate the universe. Not all of us can do that. Drugs might be the best way, dope yourself up on Morphine, but that wouldn't do because in the end, all you become is some slimy mess living in your own vomit in some deep and dark alleyway. No where to go, or to say.

Repetition, AGAIN, doing it again and again, the daily matters of life, doing them rote and being bored in the process.

But life has always been a matter of repetition, true, repetition in eating and sleeping and excreting and sexing and the like, and in the end, there is an absence of feeling there. AGAIN and AGAIN and on top of all of that, there is the free time; repetition and free time thereafter, the killer of the soul as I see it, the killer of my soul. Give me one person that isn't stimulated beyond boredom and I will give you one unhappy person in search of a life. Where does this lead me? Where does this lead anyway. I suffer greatly with all this, suffer terribly.

I am an unemployed adult male in search of a life!

## CONCLUDING THE CONCLUSION

Unemployed for months and many more after the completion of my daily diary. There would be many more days of loneliness, many more days of waiting by the phone and hearing nothing more from employers, many more days of self-evaluation and wondering. Time, piercing my heart, breaking my heart, taking all of my strength away, months and still nothing concrete, no job offers, no place to go, time, months, and with the passing time, passing self-confidence, wonderment at what exactly I can do anymore, exactly what I can offer an employer, exactly what I can offer anybody anywhere.

And the day I do finally get an interview, there is a big bang in New York City; terrorists have blown up the world trade center. The nation's Recession now turns into a Depression and my interview is cancelled as thousands of human beings are buried to death, squashed under metal beams and concrete, cooked with fire, etc., so on, so forth. There will be no jobs for me now or in the foreseeable future. Who will hire me? I don't know. Who will want me? I don't know. What should I do? I don't know. Disaster around me and disaster happening personally. It all looks bleak to me, but I push on. Having children makes you push on.

I will eventually get a job and then maybe another and then maybe another and then maybe another and then I will be closer enough to retirement and then I will have no money to retire and then I will be at the mercy of other people and they will do with me what they want to do with me, that is, if I don't perish before the final fall. It is a dismal sequence of events but I cannot see anything but dismal out there.

The World Trade Center bombing, thousands gone, and people that I used to work with missing, dead, gone, perished. These were hard working souls who gave years to their company - where I met them - asked for not much, a vacation or so a year, paid their mortgages, ate out occasionally, etc., etc., etc. In other words, they were better people then I, ever, better and more responsible, better employees, better values, better in general, and in return they were flayed alive and every bone in their body was broken and dismembered. What makes sense and what doesn't make sense?

But maybe this unemployment thing has been good. It has made me focus on the other side of life, it has made me see the other side and how the people on the other side live and work and struggle. This unemployment thing has given me the opportunity, the isolation to garner my thoughts and understand my place in the world and the world of others. This is good, right? Or, I might be justifying, merely justifying, or merely making excuses, or, merely alibying, or, trying to paint a pretty picture over a truly ugly canvas. Who knows?

So no job, that's what it leads to in the end; and the economy is only getting worse, which means no job in the future of time. Mentally, I ask myself, how long can I hold out, how long can I hold out depression and depressing thoughts. There is worry about this depression, about going into it and never coming out of it. To pull yourself up and out into the brightest sunshine is a difficult task, almost like a drug addict pulling away from their drugs. Depression is addictive; it is a comfortable place to travel within, and when one is depressed, facing depression, one is freed, one is unburdened. The normal course of events do not exist, the normal responsibilities do not exist. Depression takes you to another world somewhere beyond. Trouble is whether this other world is the real world, or a world that is just as false as the real one. Interesting.

Back to the unemployment blues, depression, a country's depression, looking around for employers, being isolated in the suburbs, searching for relevance where relevancy does not exist, looking for meaning in ideas where ideas are false and barren, seeking to hold on when there is no tree, no hanging branches to clutch on to, always waiting, expecting the call when there are no calls, nobody wants to call, nobody wants to care. Unemployment, feelings, thoughts, feeling oppressed, wanting to be the oppressor, so many things pop into the head and then out. It is an amazing spectacle, amazing indeed. Energy expended in visions of what is, what was, what can be, energy burned, gone forever, burned but never used as fuel. It is a waste, a colossal waste. Or, is it?

This time of life is never to be forgotten. That is a promise!

END!

www.ingramcontent.com/pod-product-compliance
Lightning Source LLC
Chambersburg PA
CBHW070137290526
45789CB00002B/523